Cats, Rats & Other Creatures

15 Patterns & Design Techniques

Cats, Rats & Other Creatures

15 Patterns & Design Techniques

Neysa A. Phillippi

Reverie

PUBLISHING COMPANY

Dedications

I dedicate this book, which would not have been possible without
a warped imagination and my avid collectors, to:

My husband Gerry McKinney, for his continuing support of my
individuality and his passing comments about my creations

Bill Hippchen, "the artists' best friend"; without him I'd be computer illiterate and totally insane

Terry Hayes, the best of the best

Acknowledgements

I thank the artists and suppliers for their invaluable tips, hints and sources,
which have made this book informative and the patterns fun to make.

I thank, also, Audrey, my Waldenbooks expert, for her help with my research.

First edition/First printing

To purchase additional copies of this book, please contact:
Reverie Publishing Company, 130 Wineow Street, Cumberland, MD 21502
888-721-4999

Library of Congress Control Number 2004090402
ISBN 1-932485-13-9

Project Editor: Joan Muyskens Pursley
Design & Production: Tammy S. Blank
Cover Design: Tammy S. Blank
Photography and drawings: Neysa A. Phillippi
Page 2: Standing Cat; Page 5: Dudley the Rat

Printed and bound in Korea

Contents

Patterns

Introduction

By the spring of 2004, more than sixty of my patterns had been published. My first book, *Whimsical Teddy Bears—15 Patterns & Design Techniques*, had been in print for three years, and my tour business had entered its eleventh year. I never would have thought this possible when I began making bears twenty-one years ago.

A lot has changed since I wrote *Whimsical Teddy Bears*. The industry, the artists and the designs have changed drastically. The current economic conditions have resulted in many artists retiring to find "real" jobs. Collectors are buying conservatively and many are making their own bears.

The teddy bear's longevity in the collector market is surprising to me. As an artist and collector, my tastes have changed through the years. I collect a specific item, then find myself moving on to something else. However, the teddy bear—now more than one hundred years old—and teddy bear collecting are obviously here to stay.

Teddy bear collectors, no matter what the economy, collect; but when the stock market and world economy dictate caution, we turn inward and begin making our own stuffed animals. We invest in supplies and patterns rather than buying the bear artists' creations. This extension to the hobby of collecting has led to many books about bear making. Now it's time for the teddy bear's "friends" to emerge—to enter this uncertain world and help the teddy bear spread love.

I personally have added manufactured miniatures, woven Belgian plush and other supplies to my sale tables at shows and on my Web site. I'm not alone; many other once-independent artists are now relying on teddy-related products, the Internet and often a 9-to-5 job to supplement their teddy bear businesses. Artists' passions to create survive and thrive, no mater what the economic situation.

I have a love—a passion—for animals, whether they are our Siamese cats or the countless birds, deer, squirrels, opossums, raccoons, skunks and sometimes bears that daily visit our ninety-six-quart feeder. Growing up on a farm, taking care of the misfits and an imagination that runs wild have led me to this career of designing and making teddy bears and assorted other creatures. This career has been rewarding—rich in friends, travel and an expanding knowledge of the world.

Although I am passionate about all animals, cats rule, at least in our home. My husband and I are second best to three Siamese cats: Indy, Ayla and Brody.

While I love making teddy bears, I also enjoy making other creatures, and cats and rats are my favorites. Mohawks and earrings, whiskers and tails, hooves and worms that squirm—why limit your imagination to bears?

Since I began selling patterns for my teddy bears, I've been asked many times when I would publish patterns for my cats, rats and other animals. In 2002, I did just that; of the dozen patterns I released, just three were for bears. Now, with this book, I am happy to share patterns for fifteen creatures that will help your bears spread love, comfort and happiness. I have included a small section on design relating directly to the creatures in this book. Also provided are special directions, tips and hints for making your creatures even better.

My cat and lion patterns are designed to be mixed and matched, enabling you to create countless versions. The rats, pigs, rabbit and skunk have distinct pattern pieces. Wiggles Worm is a draft dodger. Use my pattern pieces to create your own versions, as well. Try piecing the legs, arms, heads and bodies differently than I have; with imagination and experimentation, the possibilities are endless.

Whimsical Teddy Bears—15 Patterns & Design Techniques works well as a companion book for these patterns. It offers design techniques that work for all sorts of creatures, as well as the bears featured in the book. *Costumed Teddy Bears—14 Patterns for Bears in Body Suits*, by Celia Baham, is also a great companion book. It teaches you how to incorporate clothing into your designs. Both of these books were published by Portfolio Press and are now available from Reverie Publishing (see page 4).

I hope you enjoy making the creatures in this book as much as I have, and remember your imagination!

From Idea to Design

Where do ideas come from? I find the best source for ideas are books—books of all kinds, ranging from children's picture books to books about animals and even horror books. Encyclopedias on animals provide excellent photographs; study the animals shown in them, their conformation, posturing and coloration.

Never do I replicate a copyrighted character, however, and neither should you. Use books for ideas only—to get the wheels turning in your brain. I let my mind go in all kinds of directions, and end up with a creature that looks nothing like the art that inspired it.

Most of my creatures are based on real animals, or mutated ones. Anything from my Siamese cats and their antics, my misfit pets of childhood and photos of all kinds provide inspiration.

Consider the human form. Can you incorporate it into your designs? People watching is a good way to get ideas. Visit your local café, have a cappuccino and observe. We all have little quirks that give us personality; watch for them and think about how you can incorporate them into your animal designs.

If you have a box of old family photographs, get them out. Whether the photos are from the early 1900s or the 1970s, they're sure to provide great examples of interesting personalities, clothing and hairstyles. No doubt, you'll also discover some pretty wild hats in these photos of days gone by. Think about incorporating styles and poses featured into your designs.

Should you buy patterns and kits? Yes, working with others' patterns and kits will help you develop design techniques. In addition to pattern books such as this one, you'll find patterns and kits for most animals in the notions section of department stores, in craft shops, and in teddy bear and craft magazines.

Purchase a sampling of patterns and kits, study the designs—how and where darts are inserted, jointing systems, and so forth—and make a few. Visit suppliers at shows and see what's available, from eyes and joints to fabrics. As you make stuffed animals from patterns and kits, think about each step involved and if you can find a way to make things easier or better. By creating a variety of animals from various designers' patterns, you will develop techniques that can lead to your own designs.

Design classes and workshops are also helpful. Take all the classes you can get. You'll obtain knowledge from each class, and have a great beginning for designing your own creations.

Go to shows. I urge you to visit and support teddy bear shows, as well as arts and crafts events. In today's economy, it's difficult for artists to support themselves. We cannot afford to lose the talent that is out there, so let's do all we can to encourage our artists. Whether buying at shows or just browsing, let the artists know that you appreciate the time and effort that went into their creations.

A bonus in attending shows is that you can see how each artist designs and how his or her pattern pieces fit together to create a specific look. Note how different jointing systems work, what fabrics are used, and how accessories complement or detract from the finished creation. There are invaluable lessons to be learned from studying different artists' designs.

Start putting your ideas on paper. Write notes and make sketches. Date everything you do, so you have documentation for future reference.

Make a pattern. You may have to experiment to find the pattern-making method that works best for you: free-hand drawing, sketching on graph paper or beginning with a sculpture.

I prefer a free-hand drawing technique to create patterns. I use circles and ovals to create the head, body, arms and legs. (If your critter has a tail, don't forget you need a pattern for it, too.) Drawing on graph paper is very traditional and makes it easier to create patterns for proportional creatures. Working on graph paper is too rigid for my taste, but may work for you, especially as you work on mastering the basics of pattern making.

If you're a sculptor, sculpt the animal, and then use the sculpture to create flat pattern pieces for use on fabric. Try using aluminum foil to create the pattern pieces.

Sew and stuff. You don't have to be the best artist in the world to create delightful fabric animals. Your designs are only limited by your imagination. However, if you want to sell your pieces, consider what is hot at shows, on the Internet and in shops. If your imagination is on the wild side, as is mine, you must realize that you will attract only a small portion of the collector base—that traditionalists may smile when they see your creations, but they won't buy them. That doesn't matter to me, because I do what makes me happy. Being different isn't always better, but it sure is fun!

In the back of this book you will find "Artists' Secrets for Making Better Creatures" and "Invaluable Sources List," which includes some of my favorite suppliers, pattern companies, tour groups and reference books. Many other suppliers and books exist. Seek them out.

Let your imagination run free, ignore the "rules" and design something truly original that just screams at you. Now turn the page and let's begin!

Side Heads

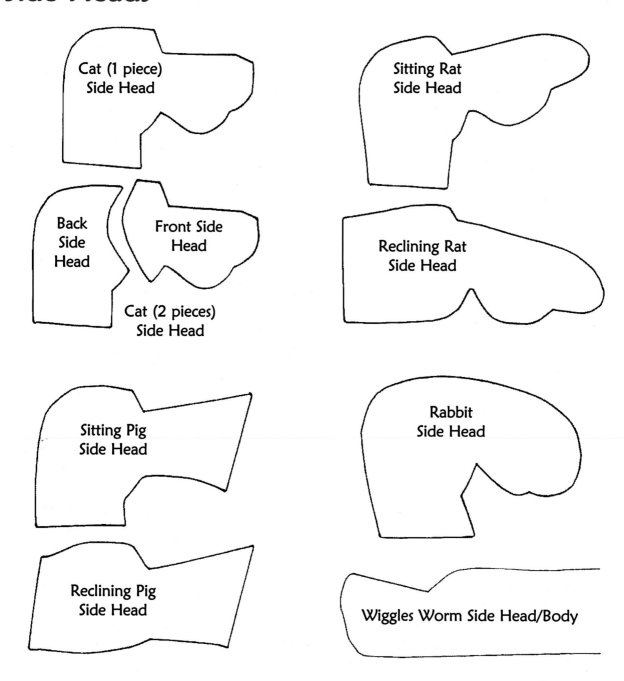

Cat (1 piece) Side Head

Sitting Rat Side Head

Back Side Head

Front Side Head

Cat (2 pieces) Side Head

Reclining Rat Side Head

Sitting Pig Side Head

Rabbit Side Head

Reclining Pig Side Head

Wiggles Worm Side Head/Body

Above are illustrations of the side-head patterns for the cats, rats, pigs, rabbit and worm featured in this book. Those who have used my teddy bear patterns will notice similarities to them, but also differences. It is the design of the side-head and gusset patterns that determines the shape of the finished head. A two-piece pattern for the animal's side head allows you to create more color variations; with the addition of the back head gusset, you can create a lion's mane.

Gussets

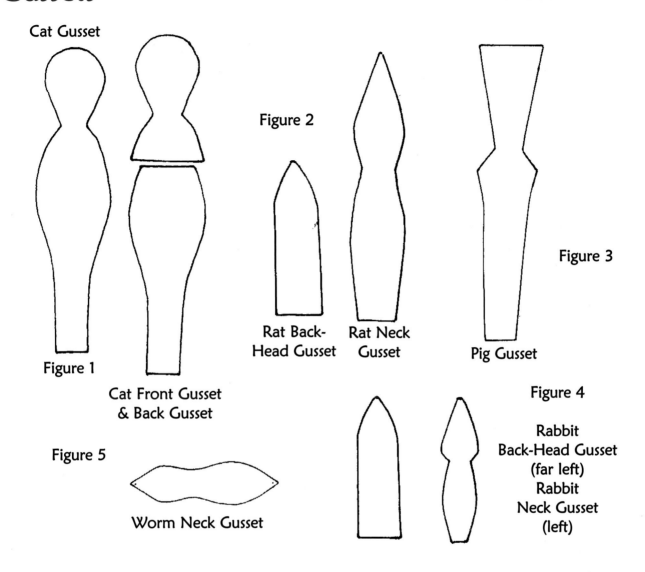

Cat Gusset

Figure 2

Figure 3

Rat Back-
Head Gusset

Rat Neck
Gusset

Pig Gusset

Figure 1

Cat Front Gusset
& Back Gusset

Figure 4

Rabbit
Back-Head Gusset
(far left)
Rabbit
Neck Gusset
(left)

Figure 5

Worm Neck Gusset

Shown here are the head, neck and back-head gussets used to create the creatures' shaped heads. All of the gussets are designed to bring the eyes closer together. The design used for the cats and pigs pulls the eyes together by narrowing the gusset where the eyes are attached. The neck gusset and back-head gusset give the rats a center-head seam. There is no need for needle sculpture with these designs.

Figure 1 shows the gussets used in all the cat designs; use the two-piece gusset to introduce another color to the cat's head. **Figure 2** shows the rat gussets. Both the neck and back-head gussets are used for two of the rats: Dudley and Rodney. Only the neck gusset is used for U. Dirty Rat's head. All three rats, however, have center-head seams. **Figure 3** depicts the pig gusset. **Figure 4** shows the back-head and neck gussets used to make Harvey the Rabbit, which also has a center-seam head. **Figure 5** depicts the neck gusset for Wiggles Worm.

Ears

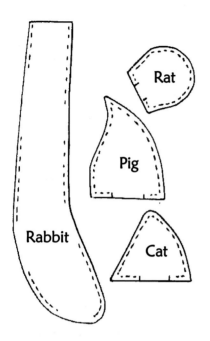

Four very different patterns are used for the ears of the cats, rats and other creatures in this book. All of the designs, however, have two-piece ears. This means that you must cut four pattern pieces for each animal: two plus two reversed.

I have designed the creatures' ears to closely resemble the real thing. How I place these ears on the creatures' heads is a different story. I do not like the ears placed evenly on the head. I believe that placing the ears a little, or a lot, off balance adds to the personality of the cat, rat, pig, rabbit or even the worm.

Bodies

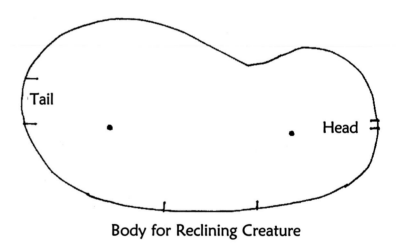

Body for Reclining Creature

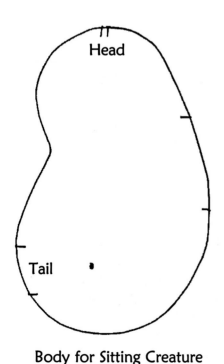

Body for Sitting Creature

I have created basic bodies, similar to some of my bears' bodies, for these animals. Illustrated here is one for a sitting creature, and one for a creature in a reclined position. Note the tail placement on these two illustrations. Make sure you have the tail inserted into the body in the right place for the design you are making. Note: the Standing Cat's body arches up to give his back the look of a Halloween cat.

Arms or Front Legs

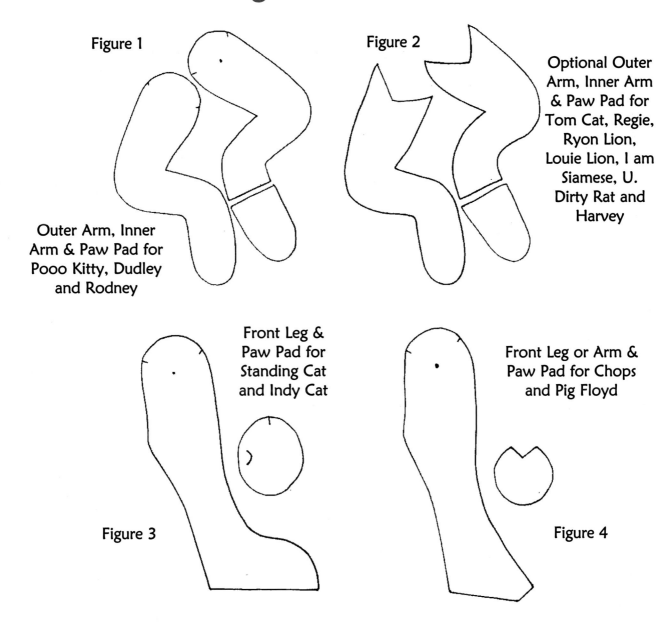

Figure 1

Outer Arm, Inner Arm & Paw Pad for Pooo Kitty, Dudley and Rodney

Figure 2

Optional Outer Arm, Inner Arm & Paw Pad for Tom Cat, Regie, Ryon Lion, Louie Lion, I am Siamese, U. Dirty Rat and Harvey

Front Leg & Paw Pad for Standing Cat and Indy Cat

Figure 3

Front Leg or Arm & Paw Pad for Chops and Pig Floyd

Figure 4

I have used four types of arms or front legs for fourteen of the fifteen creatures in this book. **Figure 1** shows the standard bent-arm pattern. It requires an outer and inner arm as well as a paw pad. **Figure 2** depicts the pattern for my "optional arm," which is detailed in the basic instructions; it also comprises an inner and outer arm, as well as a paw pad. On this arm the joint is attached in a different place; when using it, pay close attention to joint-hole placement on pattern pieces. **Figure 3** shows the front leg I use for Indy Cat and Standing Cat. Note the difference in the leg and front paw-pad shape. **Figure 4** illustrates Pig Floyd's front leg. Chops' leg is slightly different; it is bent back. Thus, when Chops is laying down with his leg extended behind him, his paw pad is turned upward; if his leg is extended in front of him, as shown in the photo on page 107, the paw pad is turned down.

Legs

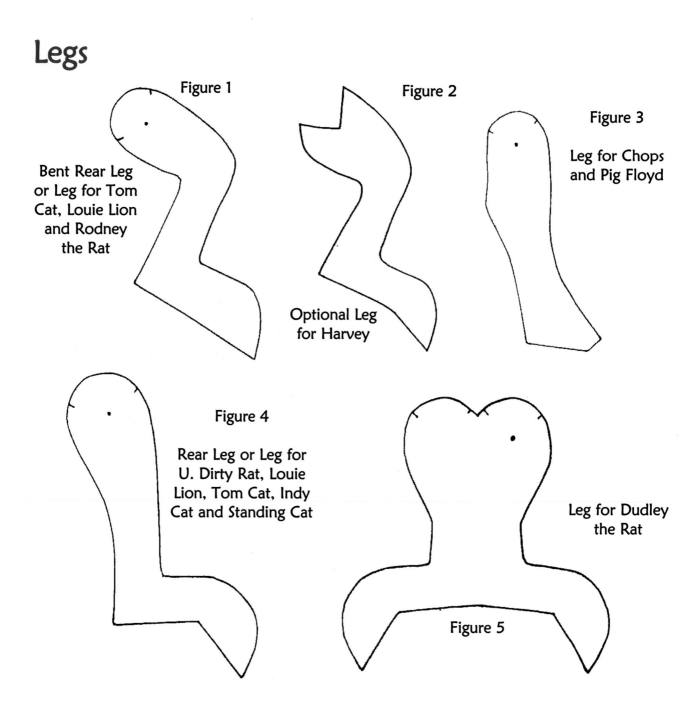

Figure 1

Bent Rear Leg
or Leg for Tom
Cat, Louie Lion
and Rodney
the Rat

Figure 2

Optional Leg
for Harvey

Figure 3

Leg for Chops
and Pig Floyd

Figure 4

Rear Leg or Leg for
U. Dirty Rat, Louie
Lion, Tom Cat, Indy
Cat and Standing Cat

Leg for Dudley
the Rat

Figure 5

There are five different leg patterns created for the cats, rats, pigs and rabbit. **Figure 1** shows what I call a "bent rear leg or leg." Note: directions for cutting and sewing all of the legs are printed on the pattern pieces. **Figure 2** shows the optional leg; as with the optional arm, use of this leg requires paying close attention to the marking and placing of joints. **Figure 3** shows the pig's leg; it is designed as a normal leg with the exception of the foot pad. Note the shape of the bottom of the leg (the foot area) and the paw pad, which is shown with the pig's front leg on the preceding page. **Figure 4** shows the design for a straight rear leg or leg. Note the bent toe on this leg; it will translate into curled toes. **Figure 5** illustrates a one-piece leg, which is used to make Dudley. It, too, has a bent-toe design.

Paw and Foot Pads

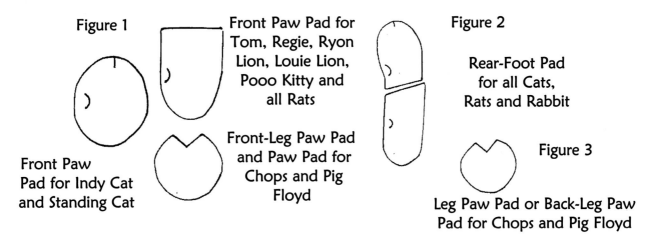

Figure 1

Front Paw Pad for Tom, Regie, Ryon Lion, Louie Lion, Pooo Kitty and all Rats

Front Paw Pad for Indy Cat and Standing Cat

Front-Leg Paw Pad and Paw Pad for Chops and Pig Floyd

Figure 2

Rear-Foot Pad for all Cats, Rats and Rabbit

Figure 3

Leg Paw Pad or Back-Leg Paw Pad for Chops and Pig Floyd

Paw pads are probably the hardest pieces to sew, but they are very important to the look of your creature. For instance, what would a pig be without hooves? **Figure 1** shows the three different paw pads used for the animals' front legs or arms. Take your time when pinning and sewing these paw pads to the arms or legs. **Figure 2** features the two-piece rear foot pad used on all cats, plus the rats and rabbit. The upper portion can be made in a different fabric than the lower. I generally cut the lower portion from the same mohair or plush I've used for the rest of the creature. I use a different fabric, such as ultra suede or velour upholstery fabric, for the upper foot pad, as well as for one-piece paw pads. **Figure 3** shows the leg paw pad or back paw pad for the pigs; it is attached in the same way as all of the front paw pads. (Special directions follow each pig's pattern layout.) These paw pads are the most difficult to sew, so proceed slowly; you may want to baste your pieces together before sewing.

Tails

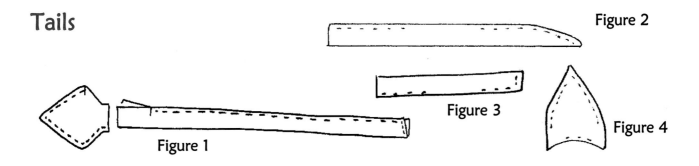

Figure 2

Figure 3

Figure 1

Figure 4

Here are the four tail pattern designs you will encounter when making the cats, rats, pigs and rabbit. **Figure 1** shows the cats' tail, which is the most complex. (See page 22 for detailed instructions.) **Figure 2** shows the rats' tail. It is one of the easiest tails to stitch, but don't forget to leave the straight end open for turning and stuffing, and perhaps for the addition of a wire. **Figure 3** shows the pig's tail, which really benefits from the addition of a wire to give it shape. **Figure 4** shows the rabbit's tail; it, too, is easy to sew; just remember to leave an opening for turning and stuffing. Special directions are included after the material requirements for each pattern.

Basic Directions

Read these directions carefully before you begin. If you're used to making teddy bears, you'll find that creating a cat, rat, pig or other animal is similar, although with the addition of a tail and, perhaps, whiskers or pointy ears.

Cutting out your pattern pieces

First, trace the pattern pieces onto cardboard, which is easier to trace around than paper. I often use cardboard from the back of tablets; it's sturdy, but also easy to cut with scissors. The cardboard used to make cereal boxes works well, too. Make sure you trace all the pieces you need to make the creature. Mark nap direction arrows, joint placement, tail placement, the head-joint opening, openings for stuffing, and the center-front of the paw and foot pads. Cut a small hole in the pattern pieces for joint placement. Holes are marked on the original pattern; pieces with marked holes are the inner arm, leg and body.

Laying out your pattern on the mohair or plush and cutting

Remember to include the reversed pieces needed for each animal. These include the side head, body, inner and outer arms, legs, paw pads, foot pads, ears and tail. For example, when tracing the legs, which are identical, you need to reverse the pattern piece and change the joint-marking placement in order to have a right leg and a left leg. Note, however, that the back legs of three animals—Louie Lion, Ryon Lion and Tom Cat-are different; therefore, you do not need to reverse the leg patterns for them.

If you are making one of the rats, don't overlook their back-head and neck gussets. Wiggles Worm only has a neck gusset. Follow the detailed directions regarding placement when pinning and sewing gussets.

Lay the mohair right (furry) side down in a single thickness. Pay attention to the pile direction and the arrow directions on the pattern pieces. The arrows should follow the nap (the way the fur lays smooth when you pass your hand over the fabric). When working with mohair, check the nap direction often.

Arrange the pattern pieces as close together as possible, always paying attention to the nap and the direction of the arrows on the pattern pieces, to save on the expense of the mohair. Trace the pieces onto the back of the fur. You can use chalk pencils, permanent markers, liquid-paper pens (correction pen) or any other means to identify your cutting lines and other markings important to the creature's pattern. Cut carefully, using sharp scissors. Only cut the fur's backing—not the pile. (The backing is the woven or knit base to which the pile is attached.) To avoid damaging the pile, take small snips with the point of your scissors. If you cut the pile, it will show on your finished creature as shorter pile in and along the seam lines.

When cutting out the needed pieces, don't discard the scraps. If you've made an error, such as forgetting to reverse a pattern piece, you may need the leftover material. Also, you'll find scraps useful when making additional animals.

Pinning

I pin all the pieces together before sewing, except for the paw and foot pads. I pin these to the legs only at their center-front seams. When pinning pieces together, push any mohair pile to the inside, or trim your pile from the 1/4-inch seam allowances. If you're working with really long pile, you'll want to trim all seam lines.

Tips

• I generally add 1/2 inch to the back of the head-gusset pattern piece to allow for the use of woven mohair, Belgian plush or knit plush. When you pin, if you have an extra-long gusset piece that extends beyond the side head (what some people call a "tail"), simply cut it off.

• All seams are 1/4 inch; they are included in the pattern piece, and are indicated by a broken line.

• Experiment with needles and thread to see what suits you best. I use a size 18 needle (designed for sewing denim and heavy fabrics) on my sewing machine, and I set the machine to take very small stitches. I prefer clear nylon serger thread; however, if you use this type of thread, you must sew all seams twice. By using this method, I have stronger seams for pellet-filled creatures. Also, clear nylon thread eliminates the difficulty of matching thread color to the mohair or plush fabric.

• If you are planning to stuff your animal with pellets, always double sew the seams, no matter what kind of thread you use.

• After all seams are sewn, but before you turn the body part right side out, carefully comb any fur pile caught in the seams to the inside. I use a metal dog comb for this. (Be careful that you don't rip seams when combing the fur caught in them.) This assures a more finished, natural look when the body is right side out. The seam line will be less noticeable. If you do not take the time to do this, you will have noticeably shorter mohair pile in the seam line, which gives the seams a jagged look.

• After you have turned the body right side out, comb the fur to release any pile caught on the outside seam lines. This also helps create a smoother finished look, with less noticeable seams and no short pile sticking out of the seam line.

Now Let's Start!

This book contains patterns for seven cats and lions (with forty-eight pattern pieces that enable you to create countless versions), one skunk, three rats, two pigs, one rabbit and one worm. Each pattern piece has the name of the creature on it.

First are basic directions for making the cats (including the lions) and skunk, and then for making the rats, pigs, rabbit and worm. Pattern pieces for the cats are grouped together; the other creatures' patterns follow their photographs and layout instructions.

Note: Tom, Ryon Lion and Louie Lion have one straight rear leg and one bent rear leg. Indy Cat, I am Siamese, Ryon Lion, Louie Lion and some versions of Regie have two separate side-head pieces (back side head and front side head or muzzle; front and back gusset).

Once you've cut out and marked all the pattern pieces for the animals you are making, you can begin pinning and sewing. Instructions for this follow.

Side Head and Head Gusset for Cats, Lions, Pooo Kitty and Pigs

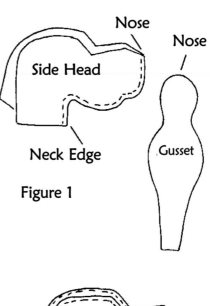

Figure 1. Pin the side heads together, with the pile sides facing each other; stitch from the nose to the neck edge or opening. Comb fur caught in the inside seam.

Figure 2. Pin and then stitch the side head pieces to the head gusset, starting at the nose and sewing to the neck edge. Do the same with the other side of the side head and head gusset. Comb pile caught in the seams on the inside. Turn the head right side out, comb fur from the outside seam and set aside.

Figure 2

Side Head, Neck Gusset and Back Head Gusset for Rats, Rabbit and Worm

Figure 1. Pin one neck gusset to a side head, pile sides together. Pin the back-head gusset to the same side head and stitch.

Figure 2. Stitch the neck gusset and the back-head gusset to the side head as shown. Now pin the other side head to the neck gusset and back-head gusset. Stitch the seams.

Figure 3. Pin the two side heads together from the back of the head to the underside of the nose and stitch. Comb fur caught in seams on the inside. Turn the finished head right side out, comb the fur from the seams and set aside.

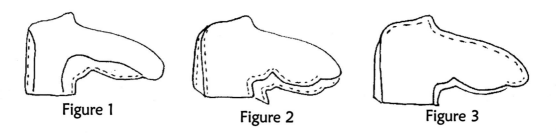

Figure 1   Figure 2   Figure 3

Ears

All of the ears in these patterns are made of two pieces. To make the two ears needed for each animal, you must cut two with the pattern face up, then two with the pattern in reverse. I am always cutting out more than one creature at a time, so I mark the ears with an X and an O (for forward and reverse). Note: I shave my cat, rat and pig ears before pinning.

Pin an X to an O, right sides facing each other, and then stitch the two pieces together. Repeat to make the second ear. Leave an opening along the center of each ear's straight edge, as shown in the accompanying illustration; working the fabric through the opening, turn each ear right side out. Now close the opening with a ladder stitch; use a long piece of thread for this, and after sewing, leave the thread attached. Later, you will use this thread to stitch the ear to the head. Comb fur at the seam lines and set aside.

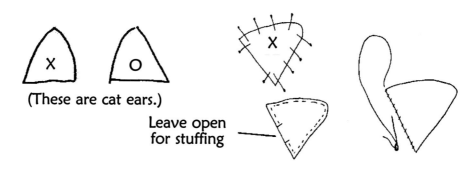

(These are cat ears.)

Leave open for stuffing

Cat Tail

Figure 1. Before you sew the body, fold the piece marked "Tail 1" in half. Pin and sew the tail, leaving at least two inches of one end open, as shown. Now pin and sew the two "Tail 2" pieces together, again, leaving an opening.

Figure 2. Sew the two tail pieces together.

Figure 3. Finish sewing the "Tail 1" piece, leaving an opening for turning and stuffing. Turn tail right side out. Use a small stuffing tool for turning the narrow section. Fill the end of the tail with plastic pellets, and then use a ladder stitch to close the opening.

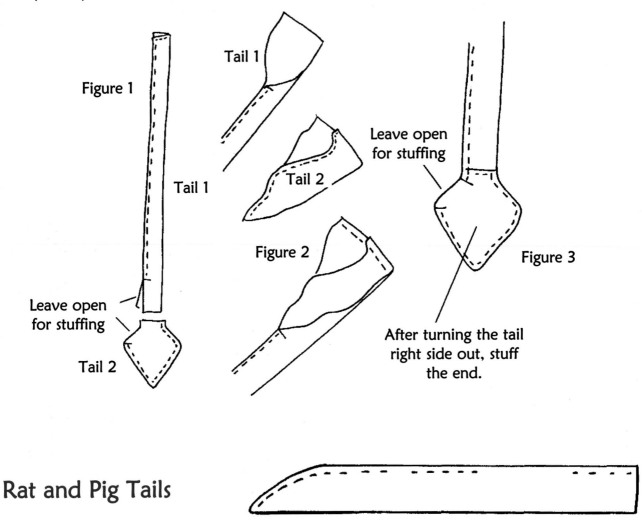

Figure 1

Tail 1

Tail 1

Tail 2

Leave open for stuffing

Tail 2

Figure 2

Leave open for stuffing

After turning the tail right side out, stuff the end.

Figure 3

Rat and Pig Tails

Fold the rat or pig tail in half, as shown in the accompanying diagram. Pin and stitch seams, leaving the squared end open for turning and stuffing. If making the pig, leave one end open; the next section and special directions included with each pattern provide information on wiring the pig's tail.

Wiring the Body and Tail

Figure 1. Before sewing the body, fold the tail as shown in the previous section and sew seams, leaving the straight end open. Turn right side out. Fold floral wire or thin copper wire in half and insert it into the tail. Leave at least three inches of extra wire exposed.

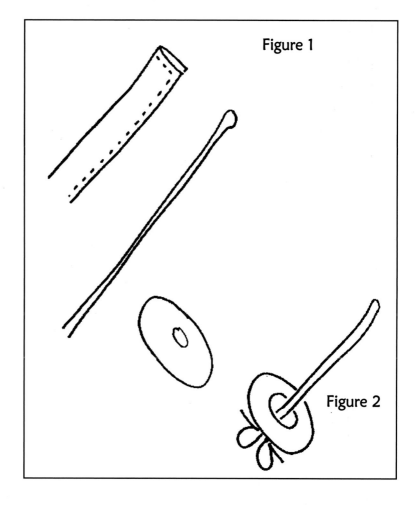

Figure 1

Figure 2

After you have inserted the wire, place the tail in the body. Pin it in place, leaving the three inches of wire exposed. The tail should be between the two body pieces, as illustrated in the next section.

Figure 2. Sew the body together as previously instructed. Turn the body right side out. You now need a joint disk (at least a 35-mm disk). Place the exposed wire through the disk inside the body and turn the wire as you would a cotter pin. This anchors the tail firmly when the body is stuffed.

Note: Standing Cat, Pooo Kitty, Chops and Pig Floyd have wired tails. The rat tails may also be wired in the same way.

Body: If the animal's body pattern consists of a chest patch and lower body, sew these pieces together before proceeding. With the body's right sides (pile sides) pinned together, the tail turned right side out and placed between the body pieces, sew the body seams. The fabric should have openings marked for joints, the head and stuffing. Be careful that you leave these sections open. Hint: it's a good idea to backstitch at all openings for added strength.

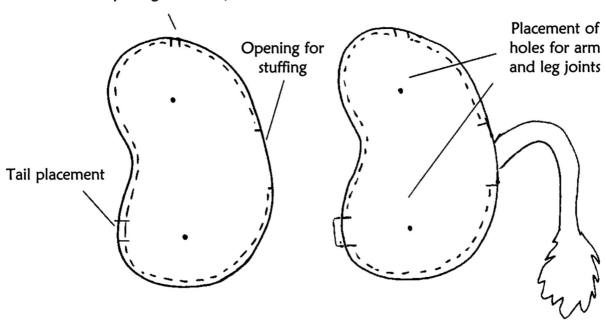

Neck opening for head joint

Opening for stuffing

Placement of holes for arm and leg joints

Tail placement

Before turning right side out, punch holes at the joint-placement markings; use an awl or the tip of closed scissors for this. You will have four holes; try not to break the threads while spreading the fur backing with the scissors or awl. Breaking the threads will create a weak spot on your creature. Do NOT cut a hole for placement of the joints. Note that your joint hole for the head joint is on your seam line.

Once holes are created, comb fur from the seams on the inside. Turn the body right side out and comb fur from all seams, including the tail's, on the outside.

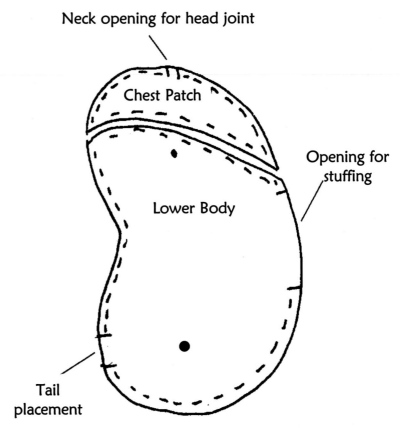

Neck opening for head joint

Chest Patch

Opening for stuffing

Lower Body

Tail placement

Normal Arm

With right sides together, pin and stitch the inner arms to the paw pads. Next, pin the completed inner arm with pad to the outer arm. Sew the two pieces together, leaving an opening as marked at the top for stuffing and jointing. Repeat for the other arm. Punch holes for joint placement, working carefully with an awl or the tip of closed scissors. Comb pile from the seams, turn right side out and comb pile from the outer seams. Set aside. Note: This is the style of the arm used to make Pooo Kitty, Dudley the Rat and Rodney the Rat.

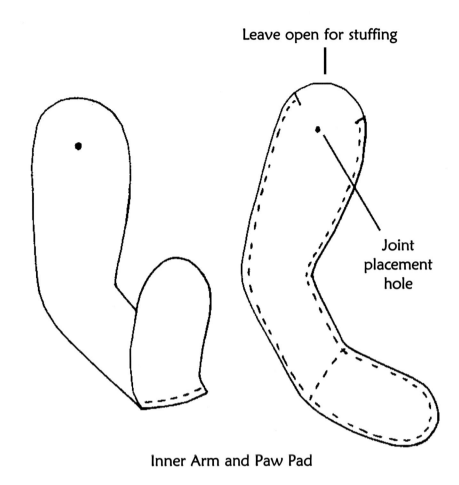

Leave open for stuffing

Joint placement hole

Inner Arm and Paw Pad

Optional Arm

This arm is sewn like the regular arm. It is jointed differently, however, as shown in the accompanying diagram. Its joints are designed so that the arm rotates in front of the creature's body, instead of rotating along its side. This design can be used to create, for example, a ballerina with arms or toes pointing in or out, rather than forward.

To better understand the difference between the normal and optional arms' joints, look at yourself in a mirror. Facing the mirror and with your arm slightly bent, move it back and forth at the side of your body, as you do when you're walking. This is the way the normal arm rotates. Now, standing in the same position, rotate your shoulder forward towards your chin with your arm bent at the elbow. Hold that position and, with your arm still bent at the elbow and rotated forward, move it up and down. Note this movement; this is the movement possible with the optional arm.

Optional Arm

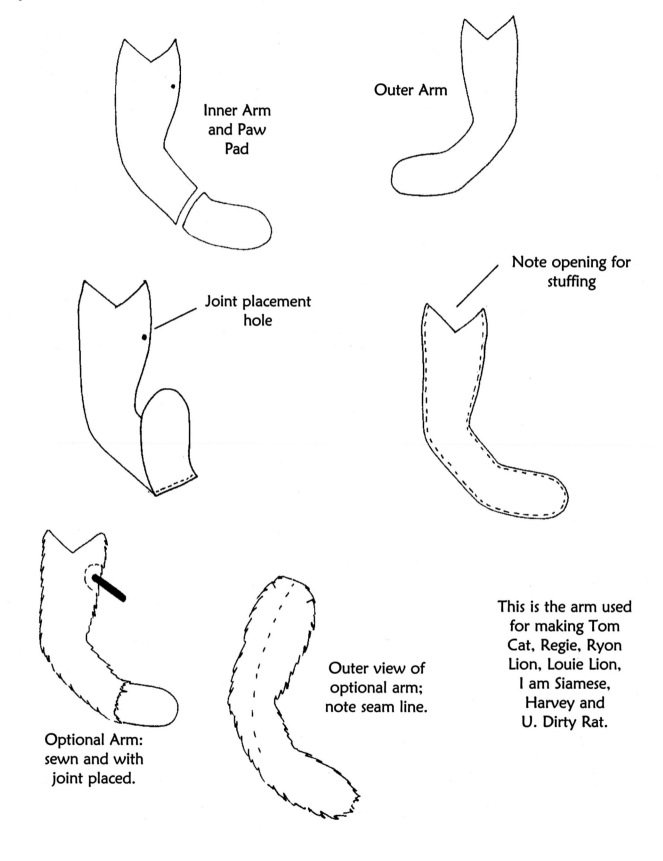

Inner Arm
and Paw
Pad

Outer Arm

Joint placement
hole

Note opening for
stuffing

Optional Arm:
sewn and with
joint placed.

Outer view of
optional arm;
note seam line.

This is the arm used
for making Tom
Cat, Regie, Ryon
Lion, Louie Lion,
I am Siamese,
Harvey and
U. Dirty Rat.

Legs—Front and Rear

With right sides together, pin and stitch. Leave an opening at the top for stuffing and jointing, and at the bottom for the foot pads. Make holes for joint placement with your scissors or awl. Remember you need a left leg and a right leg, with corresponding holes. Comb seams. Do NOT turn right side out.

Note: Indy Cat and Standing Cat's front legs are sewn the same as the back leg.

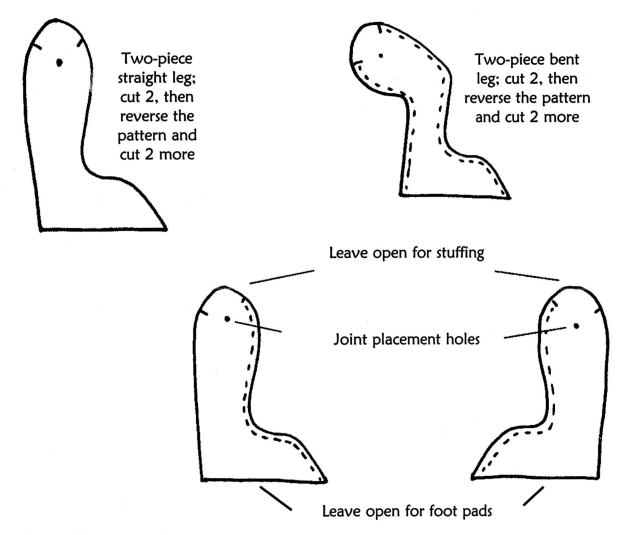

Two-piece straight leg; cut 2, then reverse the pattern and cut 2 more

Two-piece bent leg; cut 2, then reverse the pattern and cut 2 more

Leave open for stuffing

Joint placement holes

Leave open for foot pads

Leg to Foot Pad

These pads are designed for a right and a left foot. This means that when tracing the pattern pieces, you must trace one piece as printed, then reverse that piece and trace a second one. The "arching" of the pads (the inside curved areas) relate in shape to your feet. The "arch" side should be positioned on the side of the leg having the joint placement hole, as shown in the accompanying illustration.

The pads for the creatures' rear feet are designed in two pieces. Sew these pieces together before attaching them to the legs. This foot pad is used for the cats, lions, rats and rabbit.

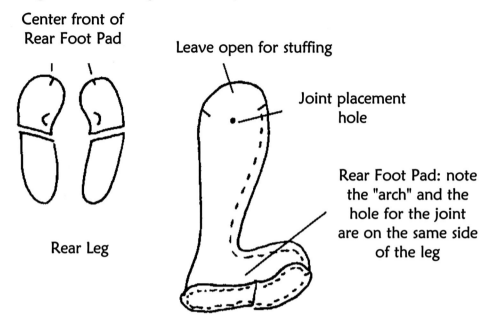

Center front of
Rear Foot Pad

Leave open for stuffing

Joint placement
hole

Rear Leg

Rear Foot Pad: note
the "arch" and the
hole for the joint
are on the same side
of the leg

Now pin and sew the front pads to the front legs, matching the pad's center-front mark to the leg's center-front seam, as shown. Generally, paw pads are made of a fabric that is different from the rest of the animal. Because of this, some adjusting may be needed when joining these pieces to compensate for stretch or fabric stiffness. After sewing, comb fur at the seams, then turn the two legs right side out. Comb fur at the outside seams and set aside. Note: this is the style of leg and pad used for Standing Cat and Indy Cat. Chops and Pig Floyd's leg and paw pads are similar.

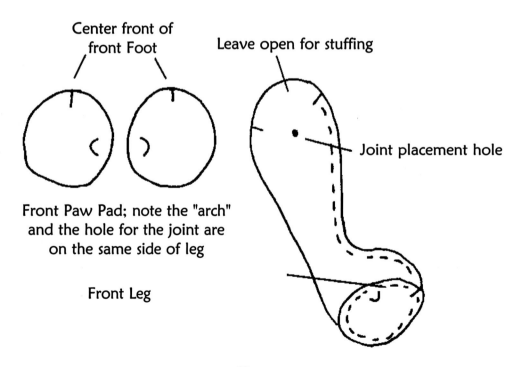

Center front of
front Foot

Leave open for stuffing

Joint placement hole

Front Paw Pad; note the "arch"
and the hole for the joint are
on the same side of leg

Front Leg

Finishing Your Creature

Now comes the most interesting creative work: finishing your creature. First, you need to determine what type of eyes you will use—safety eyes or German eyes made of plastic or glass. You also have to decide what stuffing material you'll be using for the animal.

Types of Eyes

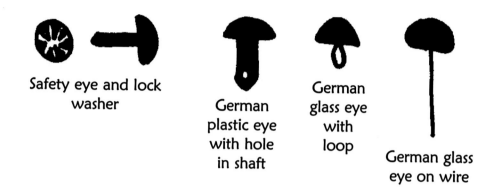

Safety eye and lock washer

German plastic eye with hole in shaft

German glass eye with loop

German glass eye on wire

Safety Eyes: Commonly found in craft and fabric stores, safety eyes are placed in the head before it is stuffed. The easiest way to determine where the eyes should go is to take two straight pins with colored heads and put them into the creature's head where you think the eyes should go. (You may want to temporarily stuff the head to better visualize eye placement. You'll have to take the stuffing out, however, before inserting the safety eyes.) Adjust the pins until you've made your final determination. Next, use an awl or scissors to punch a small hole at each pin location. Insert the eyes, one at a time; place the lock washer on the eye shaft on the inside of the head and press firmly together. Once both eyes are in place, stuff the head firmly to within 1/4 inch of the neck opening. All of my designs need to be firmly stuffed at the muzzle, with special care taken where the nose narrows.

German Plastic and Glass Eyes: If you use these eyes, or similar eyes from Austria, you will need to stuff the head before inserting them. Stuff the head firmly to within 1/4 inch of the neck opening. It is especially important that the stuffing in the muzzle area is firm. Use colored-head pins to determine the placement of the eyes, and punch small holes for them with an awl or the point of closed scissors.

German eyes have a hole, loop or wire attached to them. Thread a three-inch doll needle (available at most fabric stores) with thread, doubled and at least twelve inches long. (The thread will go all the way through the animal's head, coming out the back, where it will be knotted and buried in the neck opening.) I prefer upholstery thread, but dental floss or other strong thread will also work.

Run the threaded needle through the glass or plastic eye's hole or loop, and then separate the strands of thread and run the needle through the middle of these separated strands, drawing the knot down to the eye's loop or hole. Set this aside and attach the head joint. Once that is done, attach the eyes, one at a time: Run the needle through the eyehole and out the back of the creature's head. Pulling the thread tight and drawing the eye tightly and securely into the head, make a knot; draw this knot back into the head and pull the thread out of the neckline as close to the joint as possible, knot again.

Stuffing

There are many brands of stuffing. I use Quality A from Monterey Mills in Wisconsin. It is more expensive than others, but I find it well worth the money. It comes in twenty-pound bags, feeds out in a coil and is easy to use. This quality of stuffing has less "fuzz" to float through the air and into your lungs.

Attaching the Head Joint

After you have stuffed the head, thread your needle with about 12 inches of thread. Sew a running stitch around the neckline 1/4 inch from the edge, as shown in **Figure 9** (page 35), and then place the joint you are using for the head into the neck opening. The various types of joints are shown on page 35. The joint is placed with the shaft side sticking out of the head. Draw the thread tightly around the joint, and then whip stitch back and forth around and across the neck opening, securing the joint in the head; knot and cut the thread.

Noses

I use wool DMC needlepoint floss, available at most craft stores, for noses. Most people, however, prefer pearl cotton, which is used in embroidery, needlepoint and petit point. Pearl cotton comes in #5 and #3 grades. The #5, the finer grade, is appropriate for use on small animals; #3 is heavier and is generally used for larger animals. Wool floss and pearl cotton are sold under a number of brand names; DMC and Anchor are most often found at craft stores. Pearl cotton comes in small "hanks" (this is a weaving term), which brings me to this tip: If you have a weaving shop near you, ask if cones of pearl cotton are available. Some cones weigh as much as one pound, containing enough to last a long, long time.

With the wool yarn, I use a double strand to stitch the nose and mouth. You may choose to use one color for the nose and another for the mouth, or the same for both. If using something other than black, be sure that it coordinates with the animal's fur.

Nose style and placement are at the maker's discretion; for examples, refer to the large photographs in the next section of this book. When making cats, rats and other creatures, I use black wool yarn as "eyeliner"; I also add little black "nubs" where I will place whiskers and eyebrows when the creature is finished. I use nylon upholstery thread for the whiskers, it comes in a variety of colors. I generally use black, but for the Siamese cats I use white.

Ears

If you have followed my instructions to this point, your animal's ears are turned right side out and stitched closed, with the excess thread still attached. You are now ready to give your creature "hearing." There are many ways to attach ears; whatever works for you is the right way.

As the accompanying illustrations show, much of a creature's personality comes from the placement of the face and head elements. Ear placement, for example, can drastically change the look, as can the placement of the eyes. Changing the ears' color, shaving the ears, or changing the direction of the fur nap on the ears will also change your creature's appearance.

When I am ready to place the ears, I hold the creature's head in my lap with the face upturned. I then take the ears and hold them to the head, moving them around to achieve the look or expression that suits me personally and gives the creature a distinctive look.

Once placement is determined, thread a needle with the thread that's attached to the finished ear and sew the ear to the head. Repeat with the other ear. You can use a ladder stitch, whip stitch or the "three stitch" ear method. Sew the ears tightly to the creature's head. Comb the fur around the ears. Your cat, rat or other creature now has personality plus!

Directions for Jointing

Joint the head before you attach the arms and legs. Follow the directions for the type of joint you are using and attach the head.

A variety of jointing hardware is available. Cotter pins, plastic joints, lock nuts and pop rivets are the most popular. Some come with directions, some do not. My advice about jointing is to use what best suits you, as long as it works with the style of your design. (Jointing methods are discussed in detail in *Whimsical Teddy Bears—15 Patterns & Design Techniques*.)

Double-Jointed Head

This is used for Standing Cat.

Figure 1. Here are the pieces needed for creating a double-jointed head. You may want to change the angle of the pieces shown. The angle shown is what I used for the Standing Cat pictured in this book.

Figure 2. The dotted lines in this illustration represent angles for joint placement. Choose the one that meets your needs. Draw a circle 1/4 inch larger than the joint you will use. Note: if you don't work around existing sizes of joints, you will have to make your own to meet your animal's proportions. You will need two circles if you are using a gathering stitch around the bottom piece, which will be attached to the body as a normal bear or cat head is attached.

Figure 3. Sew the pieces together, remembering to leave an opening for jointing and stuffing. Also take into consideration the head gusset. Don't forget to add 1/4-inch seams.

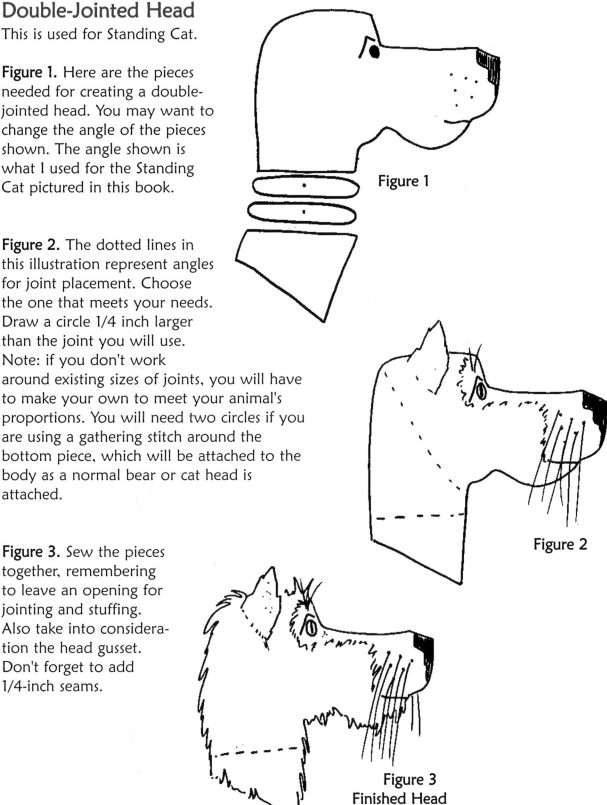

Figure 1

Figure 2

Figure 3
Finished Head

Figure 4. Pin and stitch the side head Standing Cat pieces to its head gusset, starting at the nose and sewing to the neck edge. Do the same with the other side of the side head and head gusset. Comb fur at seams on the inside.

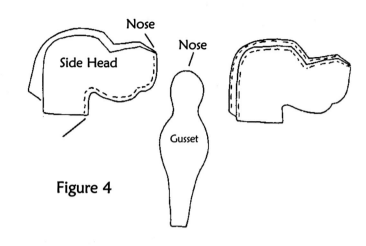

Figure 4

Figure 5. Sew the fabric disk to the Standing Cat's sewn side head and head gusset, as shown. Leave an opening for inserting the joint and stuffing.

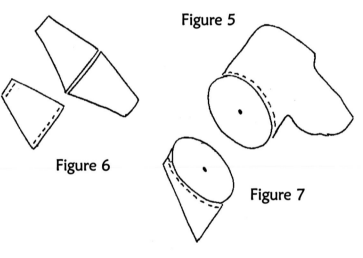

Figure 5

Figure 6. Sew the side neck Standing Cat pieces together as shown.

Figure 7. Sew the side neck Standing Cat piece to the second fabric disk.

Figure 6

Figure 7

Figure 8. Insert the joint in the head as illustrated; insert the joint shaft through the side neck piece. Add the washer and lock washer (plastic joints are shown in this example). Stuff the head. Then, using a ladder stitch, close the opening on the head piece.

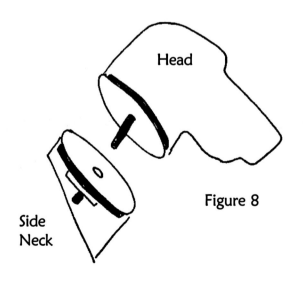

Figure 8

Figure 9. Now stuff the side neck to within 1/4 inch of the neck opening. Stuff firmly. Insert a joint in the neck opening, shaft end out. Using a running stitch, stitch in 1/4 inch from the rough opening or edge; draw your stitches tightly around the joint, stitching back and forth to secure the joint. Knot the thread securely. Comb fur at the seams and set aside.

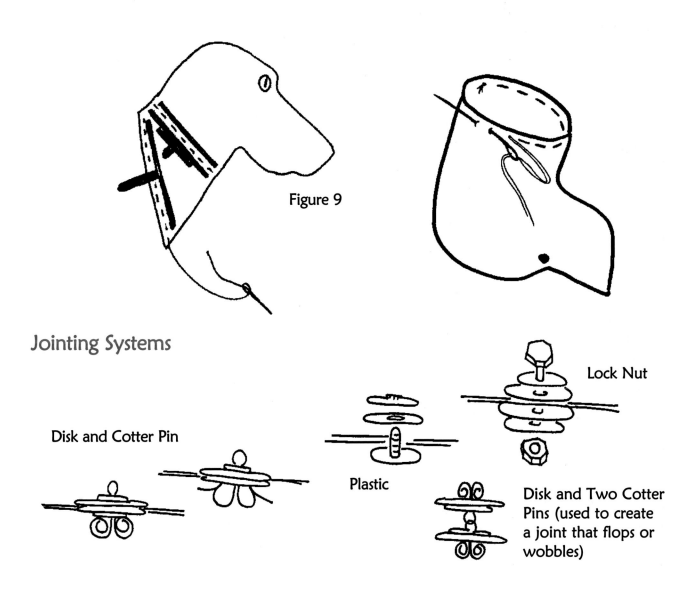

Figure 9

Jointing Systems

Disk and Cotter Pin

Plastic

Lock Nut

Disk and Two Cotter Pins (used to create a joint that flops or wobbles)

Jointing the head, arms and legs to the body

When using any kind of joint, place the joint with the shaft end, cotter pin, bolt or pop rivet extending out of the head, arms and legs. The shaft will be placed through the holes punched for the head, arms and legs, and then into the body, using the jointing method of locking it tight inside the body. Jointing must be done before the creature's body, arms and legs are stuffed.

You will need five complete sets of joints to finish each of the creatures in this book, except for Standing Cat (it takes six because of its double-jointed head) and Wiggles Worm, which has no joints at all. Joint sizes are listed in pattern requirements.

When attaching the arms and legs, double check that you are putting them in the right holes (don't laugh, even the best artists, when distracted, have put an arm in a leg hole); also, make sure that the limbs face the correct direction. When you attach the head, make sure the body is facing the correct direction.

Stuffing with Polyester and Plastic Pellets

Polyester stuffing is sold at fabric and craft stores. I purchase mine in twenty-pound bags, but smaller bags and boxes are available. I use only polyester in the head. I also stuff the paws and feet, the neck area in the body and the creature's "bottom" with polyester. I stuff the remaining area of the arms, legs and body with plastic pellets.

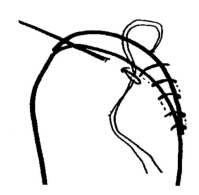

I don't stuff the long skinny part of the cats' tails, but I do stuff the rats' tails with plastic pellets. I use polyester at the top opening of the creatures' arms, legs and tummies to hold the pellets in place and to give the body parts a rounded, smooth look when the openings are stitched shut. I stuff Standing Cat with polyester only, packing it in tightly.

After stuffing your animal, use a ladder stitch to close the seams, as shown in the accompanying drawing. Comb fur from all the seam lines.

Once your creature is complete, dress him (or her) up with a collar, an earring, a ribbon; you might also add a piece of catnip, cheese or truffles to keep him happy. Sit back and enjoy this new creature, but don't wait too long to create another. Like teddy bears, cats, rats and other creatures love company. Cats love rats, so don't hesitate to make a few rats to keep your cats company. Pigs are just, well, loveable; as for worms, to each his own.

Patterns

This section features individual photographs of the animals, lists of necessary materials, suggested layouts for pattern pieces, special directions for each pattern and the patterns.

The eight cat patterns (including Lion and Pooo Kitty) are grouped together. The pattern pieces for all the cats, except Pooo Kitty and Standing Cat, are interchangeable. Standing Cat, however, uses the same tail and ear patterns as the other cats; Pooo Kitty uses the regular cats' ears, but has its own tail. These patterns are featured separately in the cat and lion section.

The "Introduction to Pattern Pieces" section (page 48) assists you in picking the right pattern pieces to make the cat of your choice. The cats' names are listed on each pattern piece, as well. To make all the cats, follow the basic directions in this book, taking special note concerning inserting, wiring and stuffing the tails.

The three rat patterns—for Dudley, Rodney and U. Dirty Rat—come next. Follow the basic directions, paying attention to the special instructions given for each rat. Different head gussets are used for the rats; they are neck gussets and back-head gussets. Their design creates a center-head seam. Note: to make a smaller version of Dudley the Rat, use a photocopy of the pattern at fifty-five percent of its original size.

Patterns for Pigs Chops and Pig Floyd follow the rats; as when making the rats, it's important to follow all directions. Pay special attention to the feet and tail.

Harvey the Rabbit is made in much the same way as the rats. When working on this animal, pay special attention to the ears and to the jointing of the arms and legs.

Wiggles Worm has a neck gusset and is the simplest of all to make.

Tom Cat

Tom Cat, from my *Alley Cat Series*, was named after a Kinko's employee. He was the first cat to have an earring, which became a recurring trademark in my designs. Tom is designed to sit; he has bent arms, one straight leg and one bent leg. He is eleven inches (28 cm) sitting—seventeen inches (43 cm) from head to toe—and has a twenty-six-inch-long (66 cm) tail.

Regie

Regie, another design in my *Alley Cat Series*, is a very royal cat: He lounges around like a king. Regie is designed to lie down, as are I am Siamese and Louie Lion. Have fun with this cat by mixing colors and making him a calico. Regie is seventeen inches (43 cm) from nose to toes and has a twenty-six-inch-long (66 cm) tail. The Regie pictured and Standing Cat are made with a longer mohair than that of the other cats.

Indy Cat

Indy Cat, from my *Alley Cat Series*, is a Seal Point Siamese, designed in honor of our Siamese named Indy. He is thirteen inches high when seated—twenty-one inches (53 cm) from head to toe—and has a twenty-six-inch-long (66 cm) tail. Make him in these colors, or in lilac, chocolate or blue point, the choice is yours. If your creation is anything like the real Indy, he'll love you forever no matter what.

I am Siamese

I am Siamese, from my *Alley Cat Series*, is patterned after my first Lilac Point Siamese, named Asia. She is designed to lie down, with her back legs either extended behind her or to the front. The design shown, which allows you to cross the arms in front of her, uses the Optional Arm. I am Siamese is seventeen inches (43 cm) from nose to toes and has a twenty-six-inch-long (66 cm) tail. There is no more devoted a kitty than this one.

Louie Lion

Louie Lion, from my *Alley Cat Series*, is a very regal cat, but much more liberal than the king of the jungle. He is seventeen inches (43 cm) from nose to toes and has a twenty-six-inch-long (66 cm) tail. Like I am Siamese, Louie Lion is designed to lie down, as shown. His front legs, made with the Optional Arm pattern, are also crossed. As for his back legs, one is bent and the other is straight.

Ryon Lion

Ryon Lion, from my *Alley Cat Series*, is the king of a funky jungle. He is designed to sit. He has bent arms, one bent leg and one straight leg, just like Louie Lion. Seated, he is eleven inches (27 cm) tall; when stretched out, he's seventeen inches (43 cm) from the top of his head to his straight-leg's toes. His tail is twenty-six inches (66 cm) long.

Standing Cat

Standing Cat is designed to stand with his back arched or to sit down (similar to Indy Cat). What makes this cat unique, however, is that he has a double-jointed head. Because of this, Standing Cat can be posed to look directly at you, up or down, whether in the standing or sitting position. You can add more character by wiring his tail. When standing, he measures twelve inches (30 cm) from toes to shoulder; his tail is twenty-six inches (66 cm) long.

Pooo Kitty

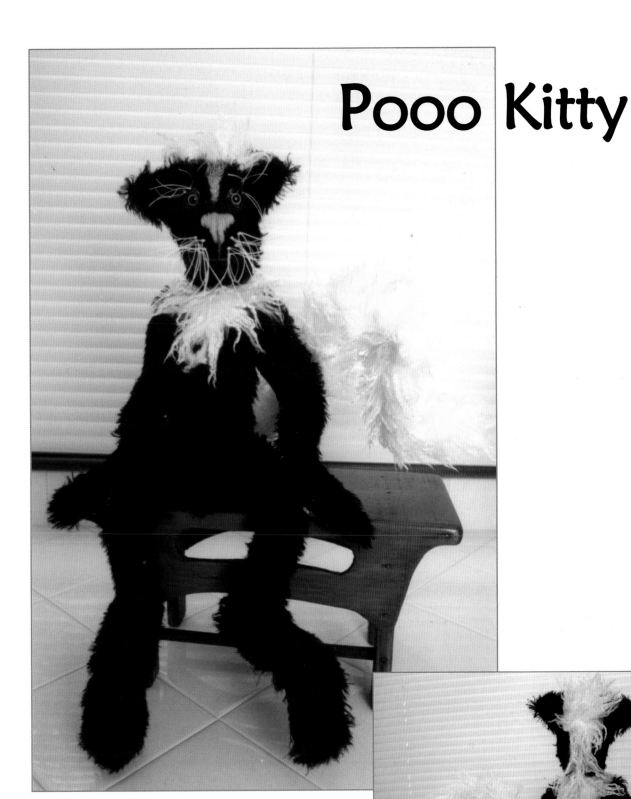

Pooo Kitty is a skunk without the pooo.
He has bent arms and legs, and a wired tail.
He is nineteen inches (48 cm) tall and has a
nineteen-inch-long (48 cm) tail. Make him in
traditional colors or use your imagination to
create a fun or funky color combination.

45

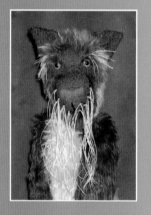

Materials

- 1/2 yard (30 x 36 inches) of mohair or plush, any style, color and length desired (Take into account the thin arms and legs; don't use furs that are too dense.)
- 9-inch-square of velour upholstery fabric, felt, ultra suede or other fabric for paw pads
- One pair 9-mm glass or plastic cat eyes
- Yarn in two colors, for the nose, outlining of the eyes and the whisker nubs
- Sewing machine thread for seams to match mohair or plush color(s) (if stuffing with pellets, I recommend sewing all seams twice)
- Nylon upholstery thread for attaching eyes and closing seams.
- Polyester stuffing and plastic pellets

Joints Needed

- **Regie** requires three 35-mm joints for the head and arms, and two 45-mm joints for the legs
- **Tom Cat** and **Ryan Lion** each require three 35-mm joints for the head and arms, and two 45-mm joints for the legs
- **Indy Cat** requires three 35-mm joints for the head and arms, and two 45-mm joints for the legs
- **Louie Lion** requires three 35-mm joints for the head and arms, and two 45-mm joints for the legs
- **Standing Cat** requires four 35-mm joints for the head and arms, and two 45-mm joints for the legs
- **I am Siamese** requires three 35-mm joints for the head and arms, and two 45-mm joints for the legs
- **Pooo Kitty** requires three 35-mm joints for the head and arms, and two 45-mm joints for the legs

The Cats

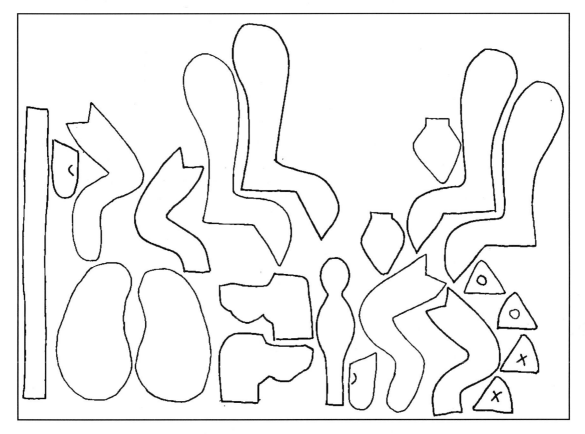

1/2 yard (30 x 36 inches or 18 x 30 inches) of mohair or plush, any style and nap length. However, dense mohair or plush are not recommended; use sparse or standard density. I use Intercal's 380s or similar quality.

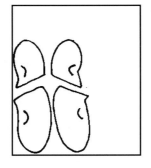

All versions require a 9-inch-square of velour, felt or other fabric for paw and foot pads.

39.375 inches = 1 meter
1 inch = 2.54 cm
1/8 yard = 11.43 cm
1/4 yard = 22.86 cm
1/2 yard = 45.75 cm
3/4 yard = 68.58 cm
1 yard = 91.44 cm

Inches and Metric
Rough Conversions

1/8 meter = 12.5 cm
1/4 meter = 25 cm
1/2 meter = 50 cm
3/4 meter = 75 cm
1 meter = 100 cm
1 square inch = 6.4516 sq. cm
1 square yard = .83613 square meters

Guide to the Pattern Pieces

The following twenty-eight pages of pattern pieces are used for all the cats and lions in this book. Remember: Each cat has one head, one body, two arms, two legs and a tail.

Each pattern piece on pages 49-65 is marked with the name of the cat for which it was designed. When you become more comfortable with the designs, you may mix and match the pattern pieces to create more versions of these cats.

The pattern pieces used only for Standing Cat are on pages 66-70. This cat, however, is made with a standard ear (its pattern is on page 50), front paw pad (page 58), back leg foot pad (page 60) and tail (page 65).

Pooo Kitty pattern pieces are on pages 71-77. You need to use the ear on page 50 to complete this design.

The leg pattern pieces on pages 58-64 can be used on all cats except Standing Cat and Pooo Kitty. However, the pattern pieces on pages 63 and 64 are used to make a two-colored leg. They should not to be used for Indy Cat, I am Siamese or the lions. For these cats, you want a leg that is all one color. The legs on pages 59-62 are perfect for Regie and Tom.

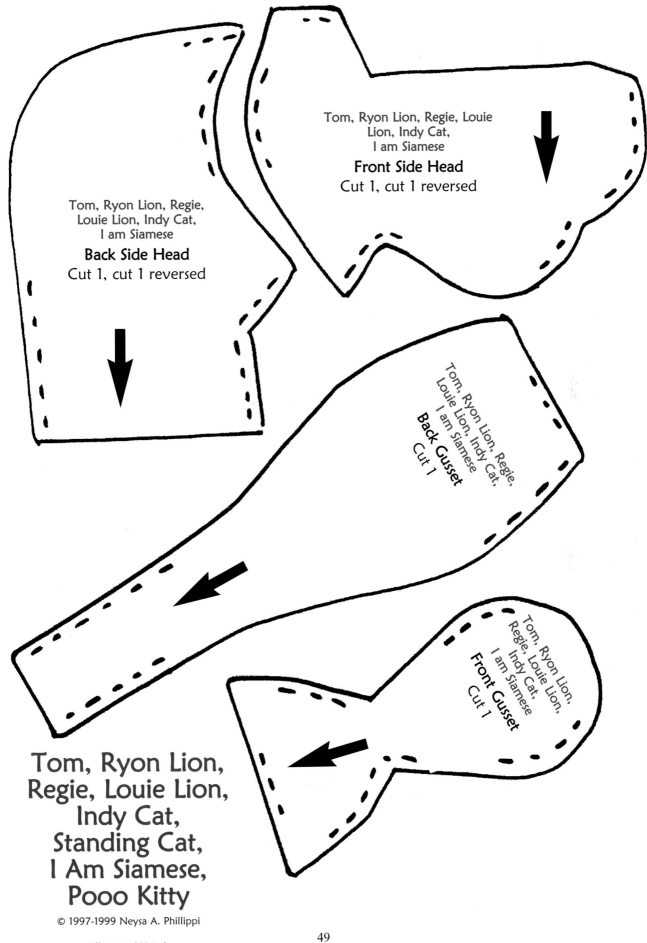

Tom, Ryon Lion, Regie,
Louie Lion, Indy Cat,
I am Siamese

Back Side Head
Cut 1, cut 1 reversed

Tom, Ryon Lion, Regie, Louie
Lion, Indy Cat,
I am Siamese

Front Side Head
Cut 1, cut 1 reversed

Tom, Ryon Lion, Regie,
Louie Lion, Indy Cat,
I am Siamese
Back Gusset
Cut 1

Tom, Ryon Lion,
Regie, Louie Lion,
Indy Cat,
I am Siamese
Front Gusset
Cut 1

Tom, Ryon Lion,
Regie, Louie Lion,
Indy Cat,
Standing Cat,
I Am Siamese,
Pooo Kitty

© 1997-1999 Neysa A. Phillippi

49

All seams 1/4 inch

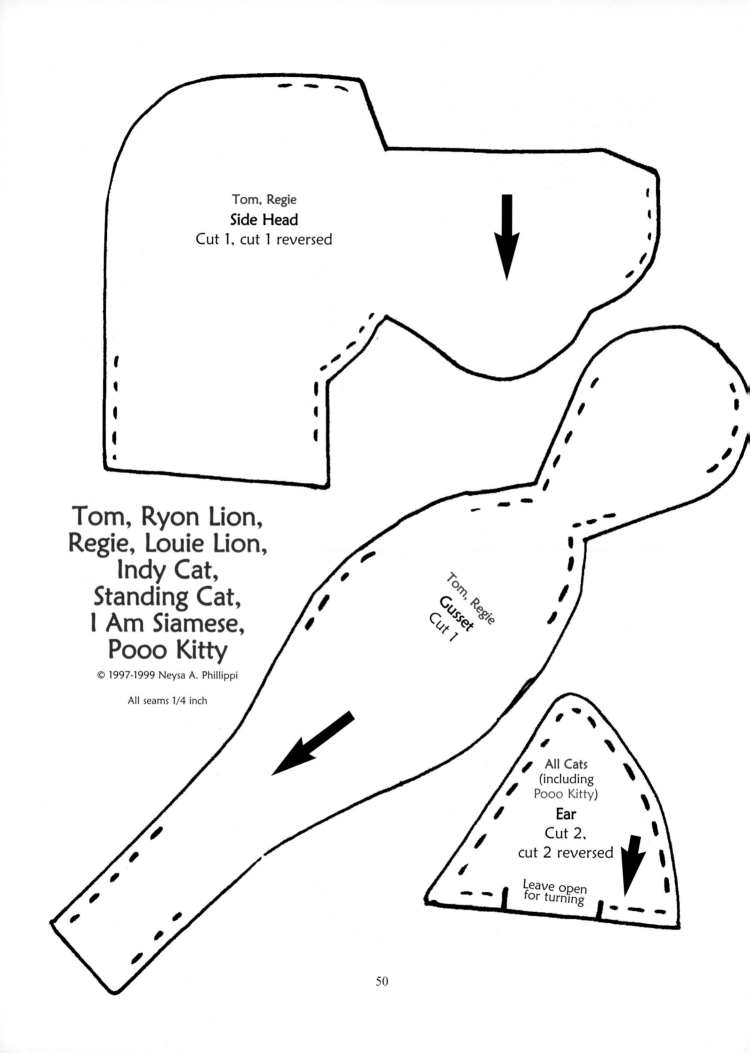

Tom, Regie
Side Head
Cut 1, cut 1 reversed

Tom, Ryon Lion,
Regie, Louie Lion,
Indy Cat,
Standing Cat,
I Am Siamese,
Pooo Kitty

© 1997-1999 Neysa A. Phillippi

All seams 1/4 inch

Tom, Regie
Gusset
Cut 1

All Cats
(including
Pooo Kitty)
Ear
Cut 2,
cut 2 reversed

Leave open
for turning

50

Tom, Ryon Lion, Regie, Louie Lion, Indy Cat, Standing Cat, I Am Siamese, Pooo Kitty

© 1997-1999 Neysa A. Phillippi

All seams 1/4 inch

Note: this is a two-piece body

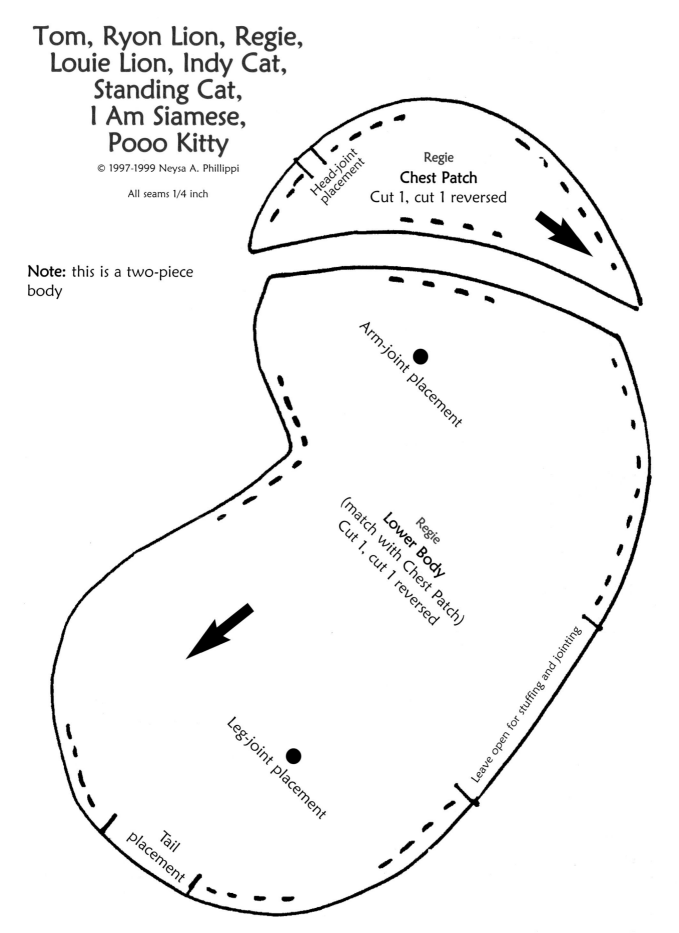

Head-joint placement

Regie
Chest Patch
Cut 1, cut 1 reversed

Arm-joint placement

Regie
Lower Body
(match with Chest Patch)
Cut 1, cut 1 reversed

Leave open for stuffing and jointing

Leg-joint placement

Tail placement

51

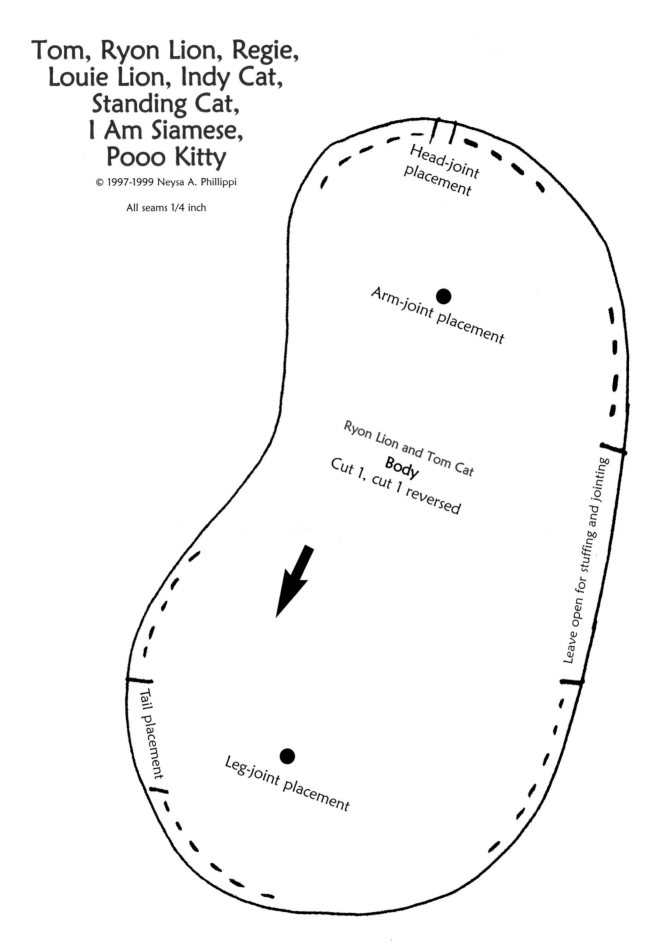

Tom, Ryon Lion, Regie,
Louie Lion, Indy Cat,
Standing Cat,
I Am Siamese,
Pooo Kitty

© 1997-1999 Neysa A. Phillippi

All seams 1/4 inch

Head-joint
placement

Arm-joint placement

Ryon Lion and Tom Cat
Body
Cut 1, cut 1 reversed

Leave open for stuffing and jointing

Tail placement

Leg-joint placement

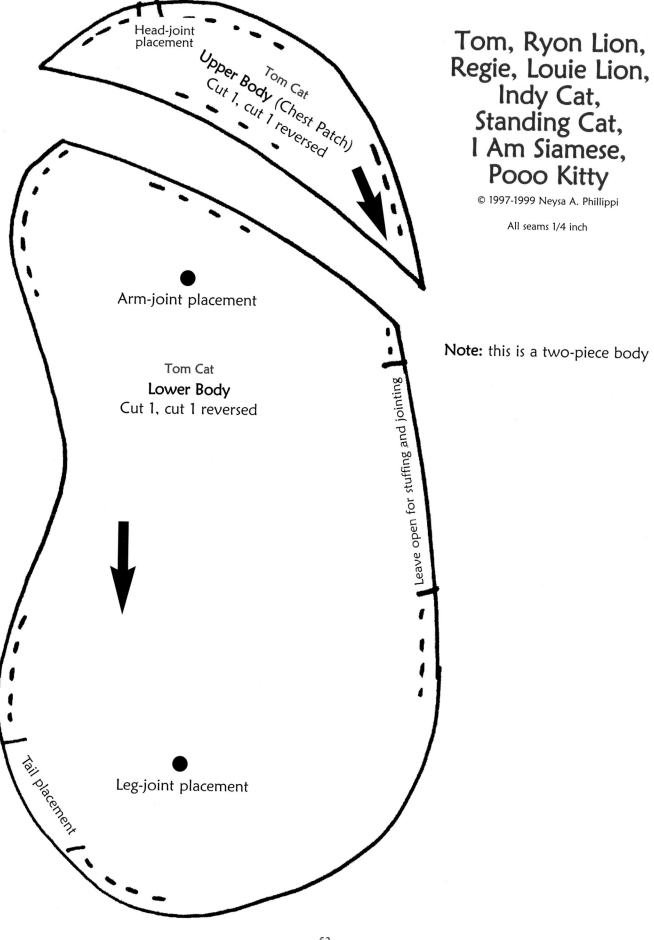

Head-joint placement

Tom Cat
Upper Body (Chest Patch)
Cut 1, cut 1 reversed

Tom, Ryon Lion,
Regie, Louie Lion,
Indy Cat,
Standing Cat,
I Am Siamese,
Pooo Kitty

© 1997-1999 Neysa A. Phillippi

All seams 1/4 inch

Arm-joint placement

Tom Cat
Lower Body
Cut 1, cut 1 reversed

Note: this is a two-piece body

Leave open for stuffing and jointing

Tail placement

Leg-joint placement

53

Tom, Ryon Lion, Regie, Louie Lion, Indy Cat, Standing Cat, I Am Siamese, Pooo Kitty

© 1997-1999 Neysa A. Phillippi

All seams 1/4 inch

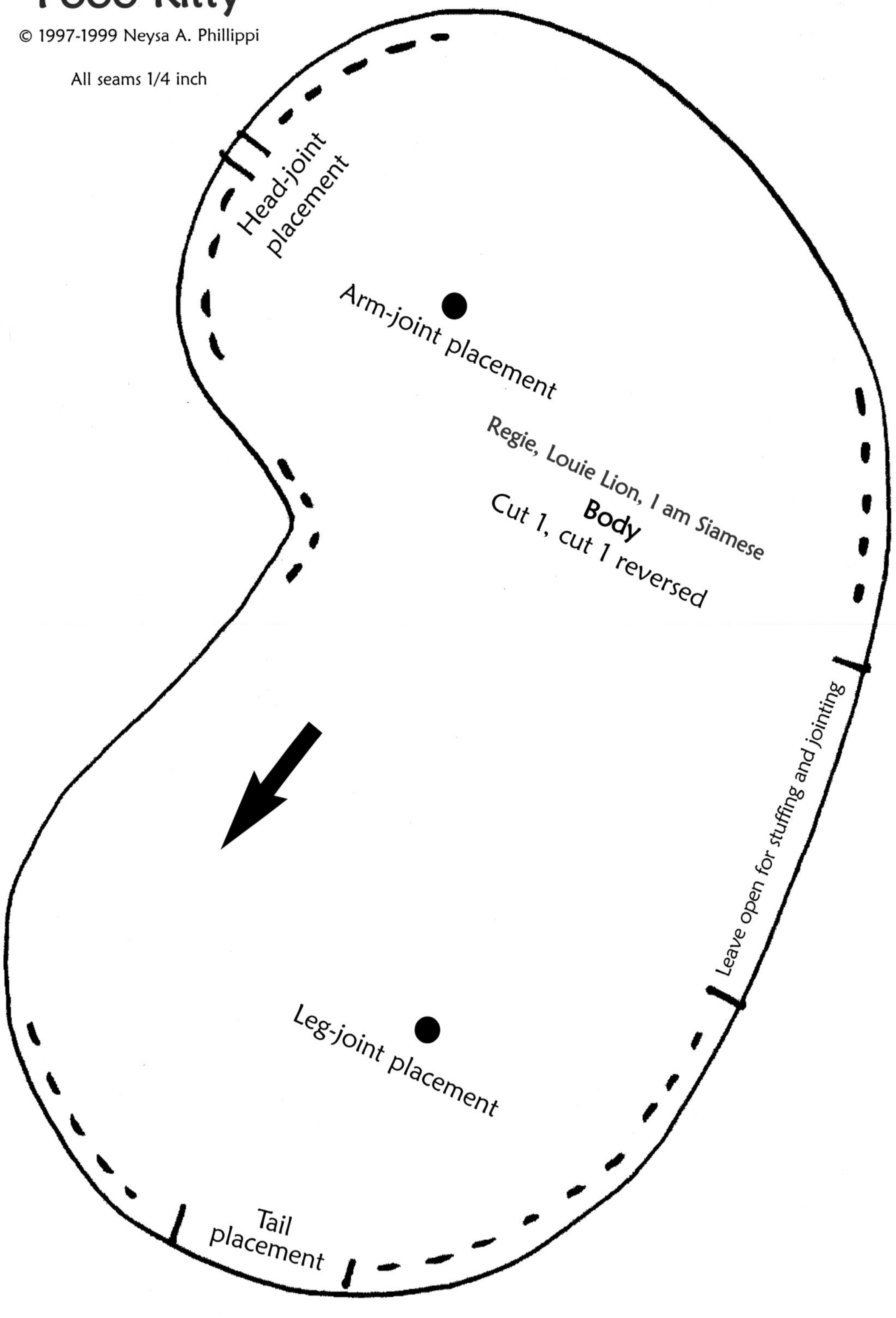

Head-joint placement

Arm-joint placement

Regie, Louie Lion, I am Siamese
Body
Cut 1, cut 1 reversed

Leave open for stuffing and jointing

Leg-joint placement

Tail placement

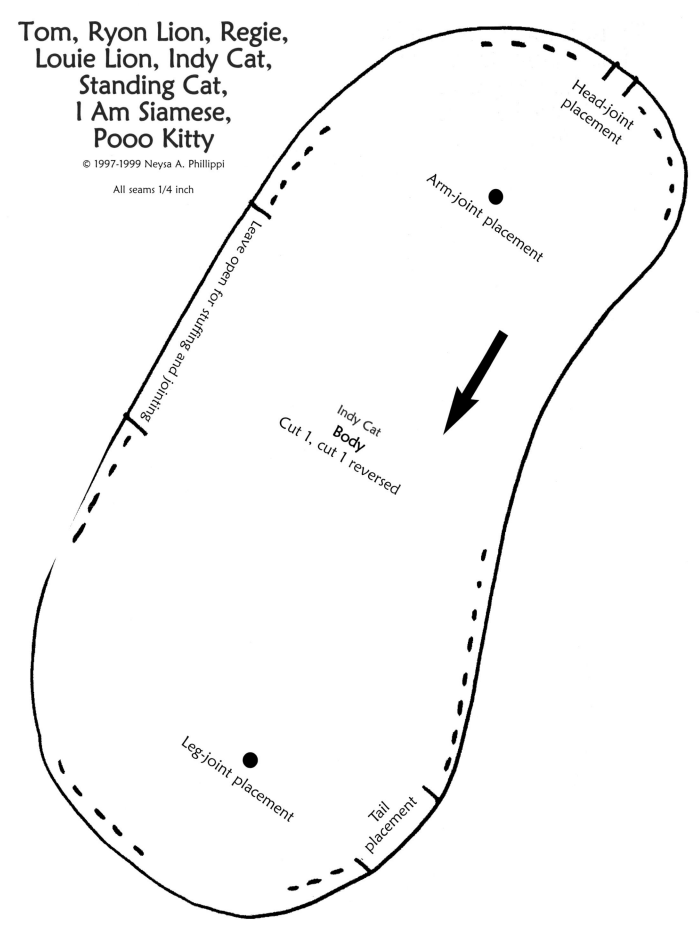

Tom, Ryon Lion, Regie, Louie Lion, Indy Cat, Standing Cat, I Am Siamese, Pooo Kitty

© 1997-1999 Neysa A. Phillippi

All seams 1/4 inch

Head-joint placement

Arm-joint placement

Leave open for stuffing and jointing

Indy Cat
Body
Cut 1, cut 1 reversed

Leg-joint placement

Tail placement

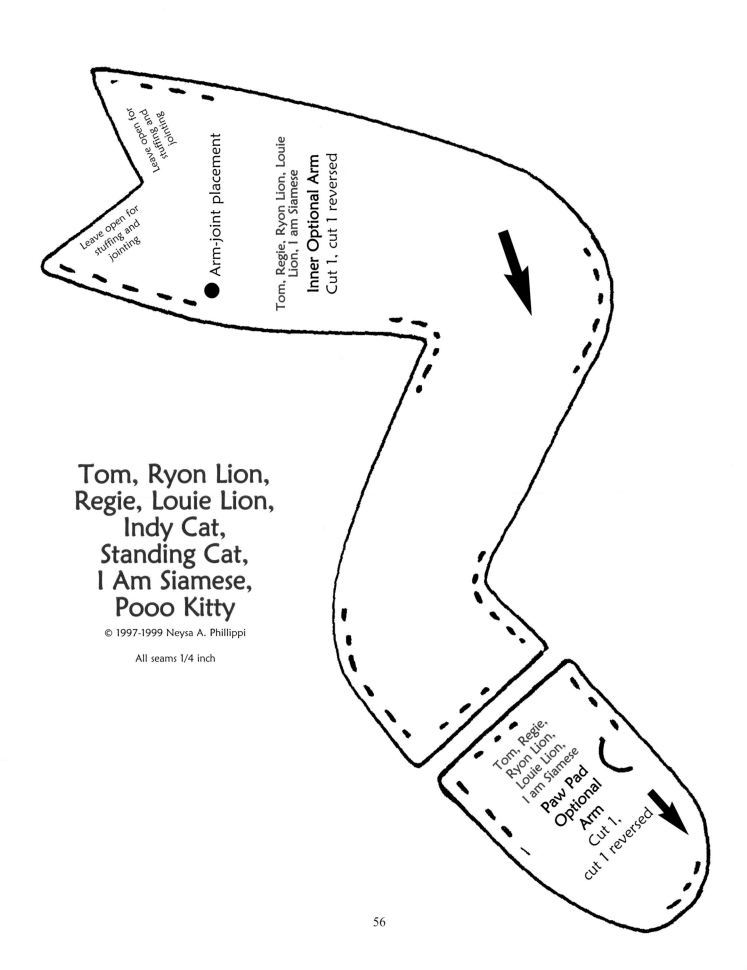

Leave open for stuffing and jointing

Leave open for stuffing and jointing

● Arm-joint placement

Tom, Regie, Ryon Lion, Louie Lion, I am Siamese
Inner Optional Arm
Cut 1, cut 1 reversed

Tom, Ryon Lion, Regie, Louie Lion, Indy Cat, Standing Cat, I Am Siamese, Pooo Kitty

© 1997-1999 Neysa A. Phillippi

All seams 1/4 inch

Tom, Regie, Ryon Lion, Louie Lion, I am Siamese
Paw Pad Optional Arm
Cut 1, cut 1 reversed

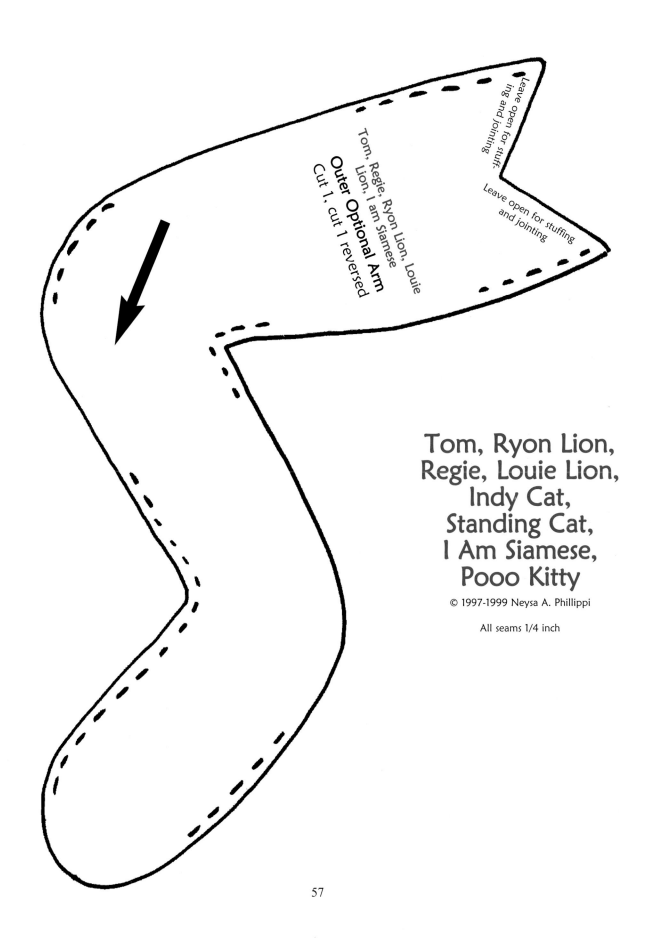

Leave open for stuffing and jointing

Leave open for stuffing and jointing

Tom, Regie, Ryon Lion, Louie Lion, I am Siamese
Outer Optional Arm
Cut 1, cut 1 reversed

Tom, Ryon Lion,
Regie, Louie Lion,
Indy Cat,
Standing Cat,
I Am Siamese,
Pooo Kitty

© 1997-1999 Neysa A. Phillippi

All seams 1/4 inch

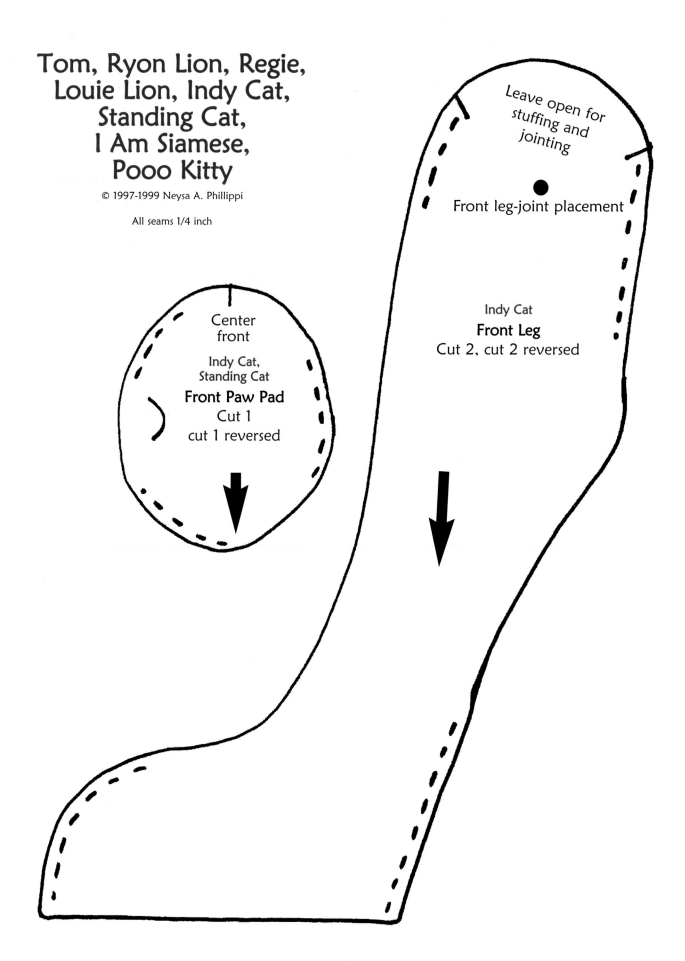

Tom, Ryon Lion, Regie,
Louie Lion, Indy Cat,
Standing Cat,
I Am Siamese,
Pooo Kitty

© 1997-1999 Neysa A. Phillippi

All seams 1/4 inch

Center
front

Indy Cat,
Standing Cat
Front Paw Pad
Cut 1
cut 1 reversed

Leave open for
stuffing and
jointing

Front leg-joint placement

Indy Cat
Front Leg
Cut 2, cut 2 reversed

58

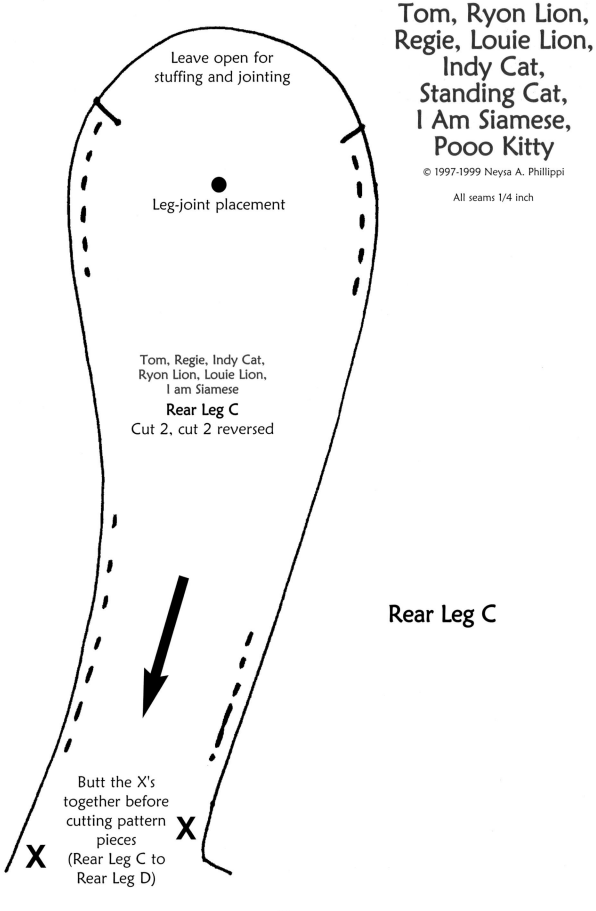

Leave open for
stuffing and jointing

● Leg-joint placement

Tom, Regie, Indy Cat,
Ryon Lion, Louie Lion,
I am Siamese

Rear Leg C
Cut 2, cut 2 reversed

Tom, Ryon Lion,
Regie, Louie Lion,
Indy Cat,
Standing Cat,
I Am Siamese,
Pooo Kitty

© 1997-1999 Neysa A. Phillippi

All seams 1/4 inch

Rear Leg C

Butt the X's
together before
cutting pattern
pieces
(Rear Leg C to
Rear Leg D)

X   **X**

59

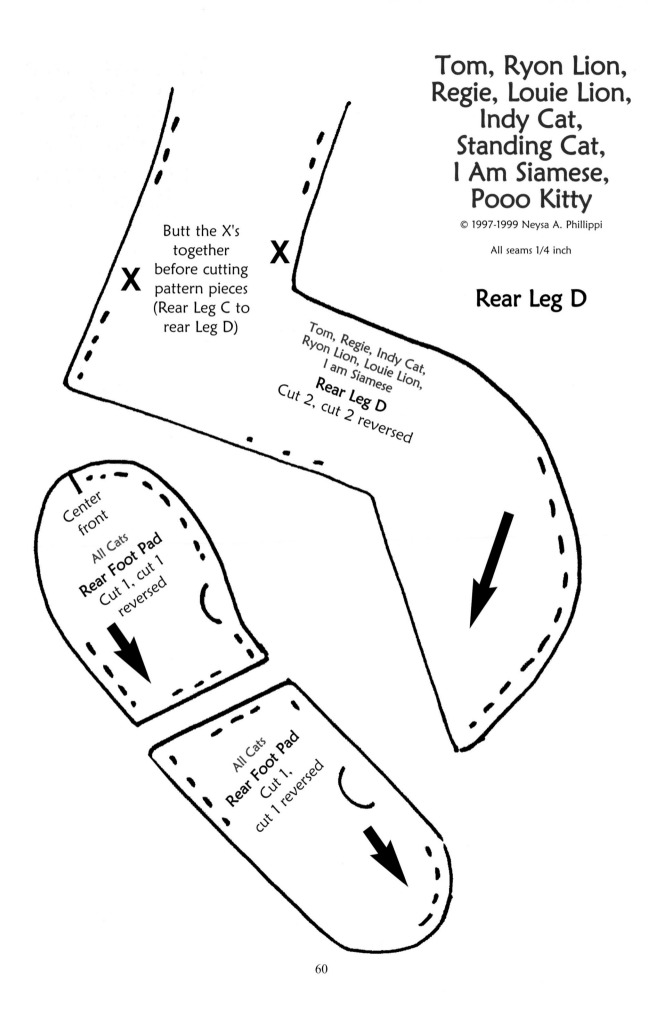

Tom, Ryon Lion,
Regie, Louie Lion,
Indy Cat,
Standing Cat,
I Am Siamese,
Pooo Kitty

© 1997-1999 Neysa A. Phillippi

All seams 1/4 inch

Rear Leg D

Butt the X's
together
before cutting
pattern pieces
(Rear Leg C to
rear Leg D)

X

X

Tom, Regie, Indy Cat,
Ryon Lion, Louie Lion,
I am Siamese
Rear Leg D
Cut 2, cut 2 reversed

Center
front

All Cats
Rear Foot Pad
Cut 1, cut 1
reversed

All Cats
Rear Foot Pad
Cut 1,
cut 1 reversed

60

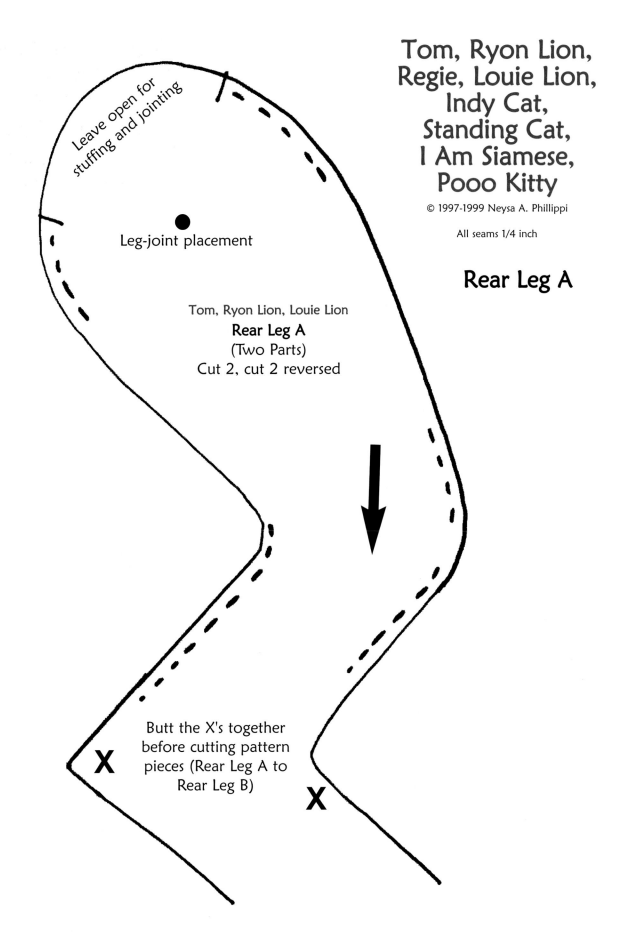

Leave open for stuffing and jointing

Leg-joint placement

Tom, Ryon Lion, Louie Lion
Rear Leg A
(Two Parts)
Cut 2, cut 2 reversed

Tom, Ryon Lion,
Regie, Louie Lion,
Indy Cat,
Standing Cat,
I Am Siamese,
Pooo Kitty

© 1997-1999 Neysa A. Phillippi

All seams 1/4 inch

Rear Leg A

Butt the X's together
before cutting pattern
pieces (Rear Leg A to
Rear Leg B)

X

X

61

Tom, Ryon Lion, Regie, Louie Lion, Indy Cat, Standing Cat, I Am Siamese, Pooo Kitty

All seams 1/4 inch

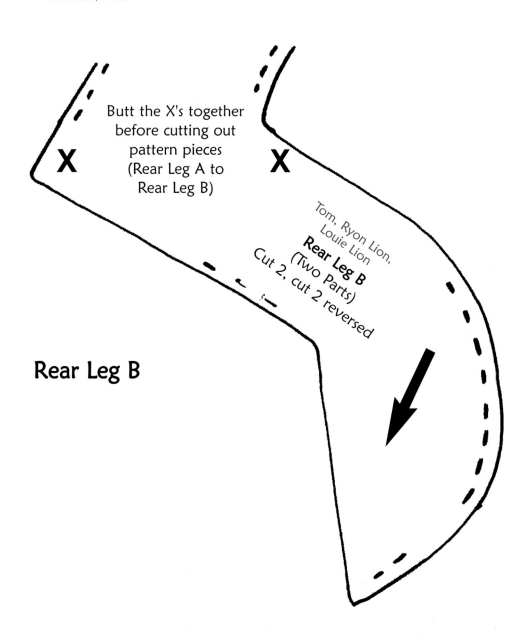

Butt the X's together before cutting out pattern pieces (Rear Leg A to Rear Leg B)

X   X

Tom, Ryon Lion, Louie Lion
Rear Leg B
(Two Parts)
Cut 2, cut 2 reversed

Rear Leg B

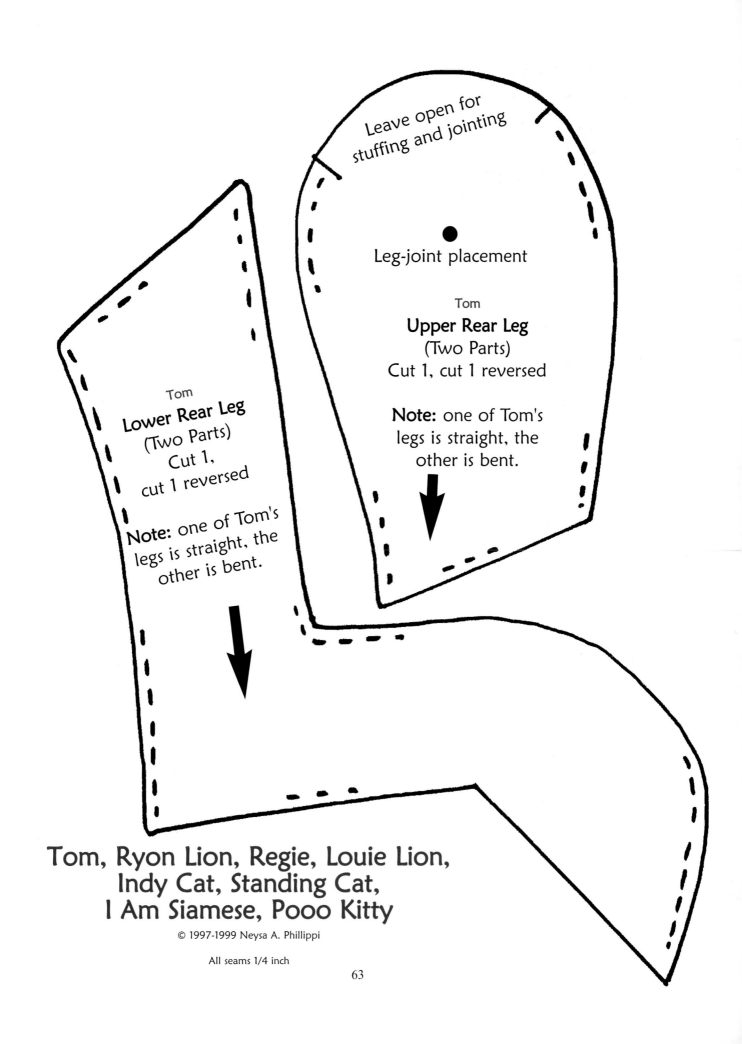

Leave open for stuffing and jointing

Leg-joint placement

Tom
Upper Rear Leg
(Two Parts)
Cut 1, cut 1 reversed

Note: one of Tom's legs is straight, the other is bent.

Tom
Lower Rear Leg
(Two Parts)
Cut 1, cut 1 reversed

Note: one of Tom's legs is straight, the other is bent.

Tom, Ryon Lion, Regie, Louie Lion, Indy Cat, Standing Cat, I Am Siamese, Pooo Kitty

All seams 1/4 inch

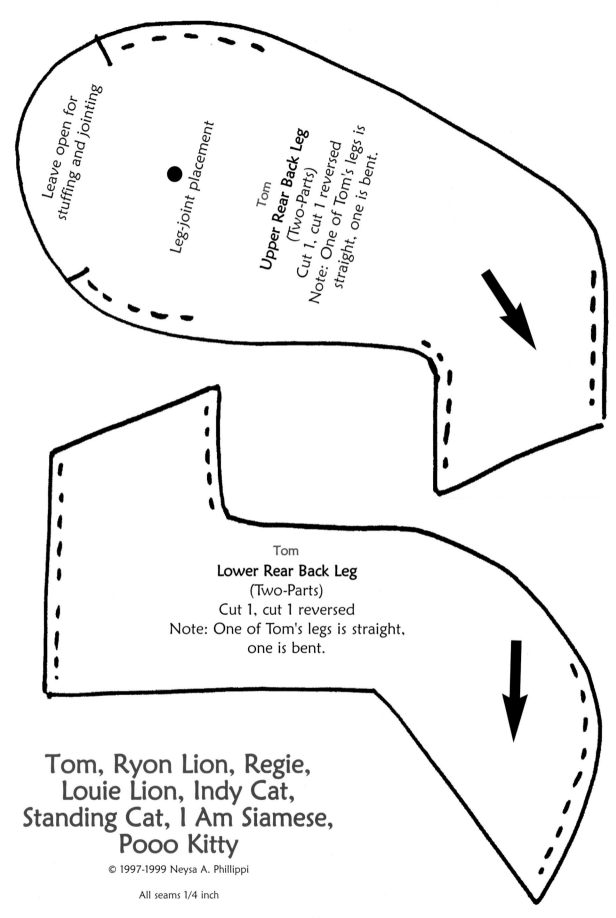

Leave open for stuffing and jointing

Leg-joint placement

Tom
Upper Rear Back Leg
(Two-Parts)
Cut 1, cut 1 reversed
Note: One of Tom's legs is straight, one is bent.

Tom
Lower Rear Back Leg
(Two-Parts)
Cut 1, cut 1 reversed
Note: One of Tom's legs is straight,
one is bent.

Tom, Ryon Lion, Regie, Louie Lion, Indy Cat, Standing Cat, I Am Siamese, Pooo Kitty

All seams 1/4 inch

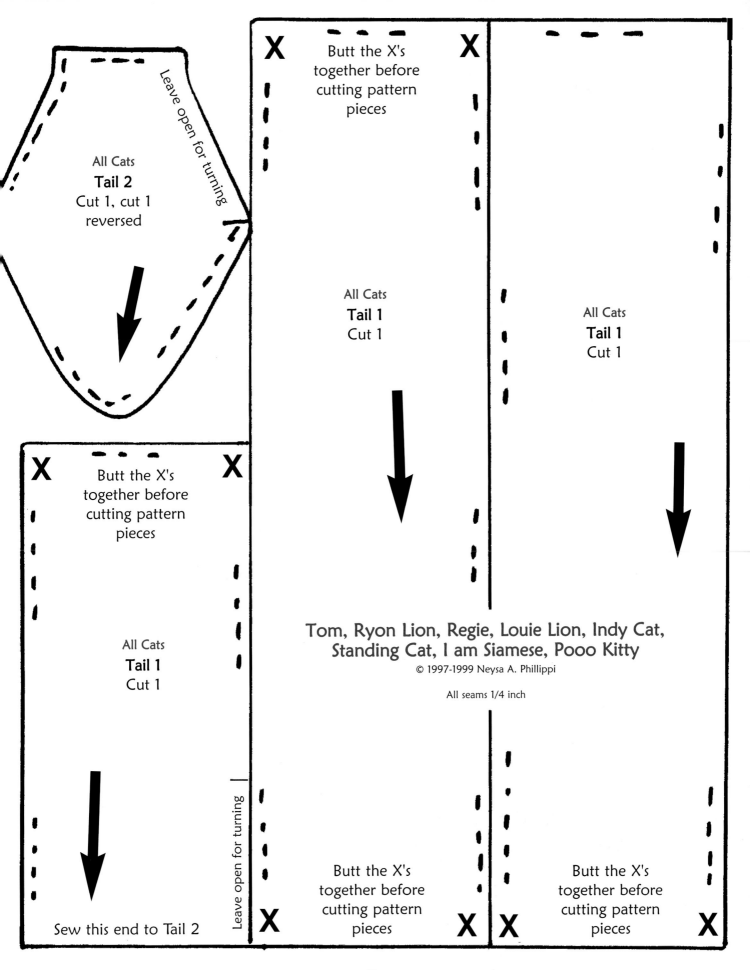

All Cats
Tail 2
Cut 1, cut 1
reversed

Leave open for turning

X — Butt the X's together before cutting pattern pieces — X

All Cats
Tail 1
Cut 1

All Cats
Tail 1
Cut 1

X — Butt the X's together before cutting pattern pieces — X

All Cats
Tail 1
Cut 1

Leave open for turning

Sew this end to Tail 2

Tom, Ryon Lion, Regie, Louie Lion, Indy Cat,
Standing Cat, I am Siamese, Pooo Kitty

© 1997-1999 Neysa A. Phillippi

All seams 1/4 inch

Butt the X's together before cutting pattern pieces — X

X — Butt the X's together before cutting pattern pieces — X

65

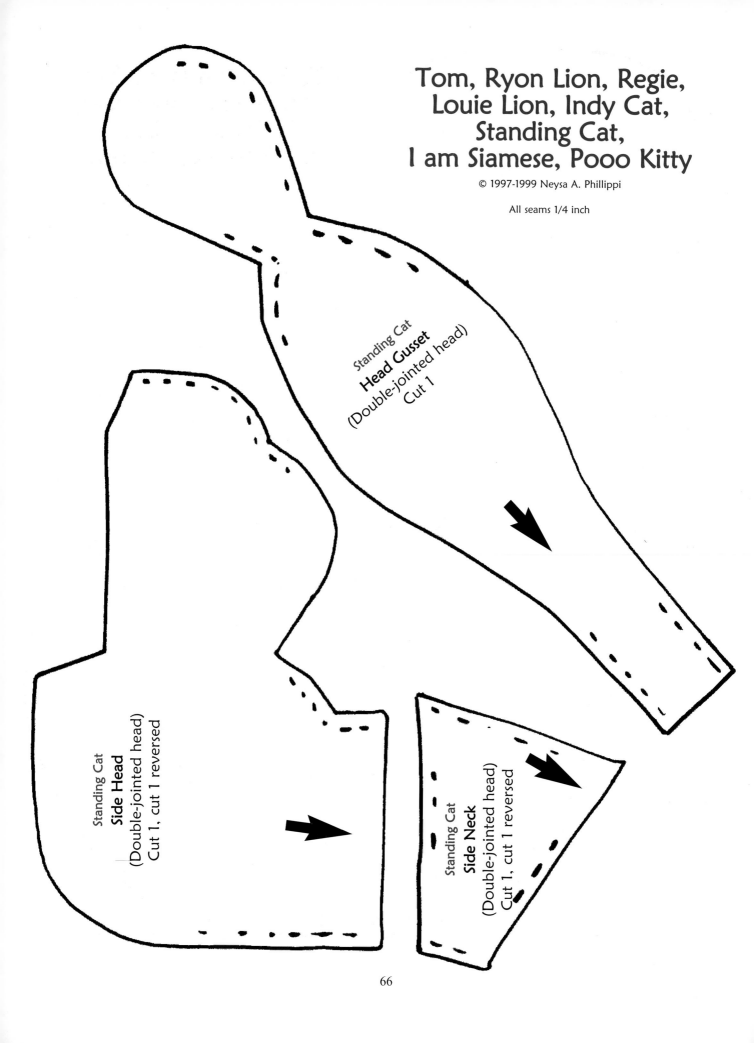

Tom, Ryon Lion, Regie,
Louie Lion, Indy Cat,
Standing Cat,
I am Siamese, Pooo Kitty

© 1997-1999 Neysa A. Phillippi

All seams 1/4 inch

Standing Cat
Head Gusset
(Double-jointed head)
Cut 1

Standing Cat
Side Head
(Double-jointed head)
Cut 1, cut 1 reversed

Standing Cat
Side Neck
(Double-jointed head)
Cut 1, cut 1 reversed

66

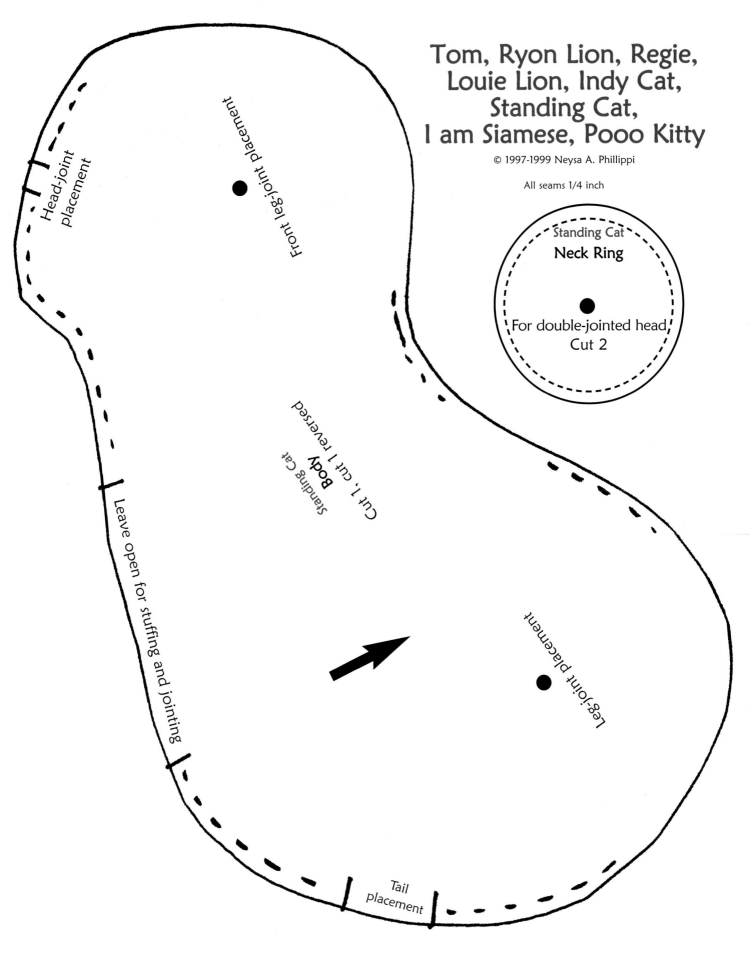

Tom, Ryon Lion, Regie,
Louie Lion, Indy Cat,
Standing Cat,
I am Siamese, Pooo Kitty

© 1997-1999 Neysa A. Phillippi

All seams 1/4 inch

Standing Cat
Neck Ring
For double-jointed head
Cut 2

Head-joint placement

Front leg-joint placement

Standing Cat
Body
Cut 1, cut 1 reversed

Leave open for stuffing and jointing

Leg-joint placement

Tail placement

67

Tom, Ryon Lion, Regie, Louie Lion, Indy Cat, Standing Cat, I am Siamese, Pooo Kitty

© 1997-1999 Neysa A. Phillippi

All seams 1/4 inch

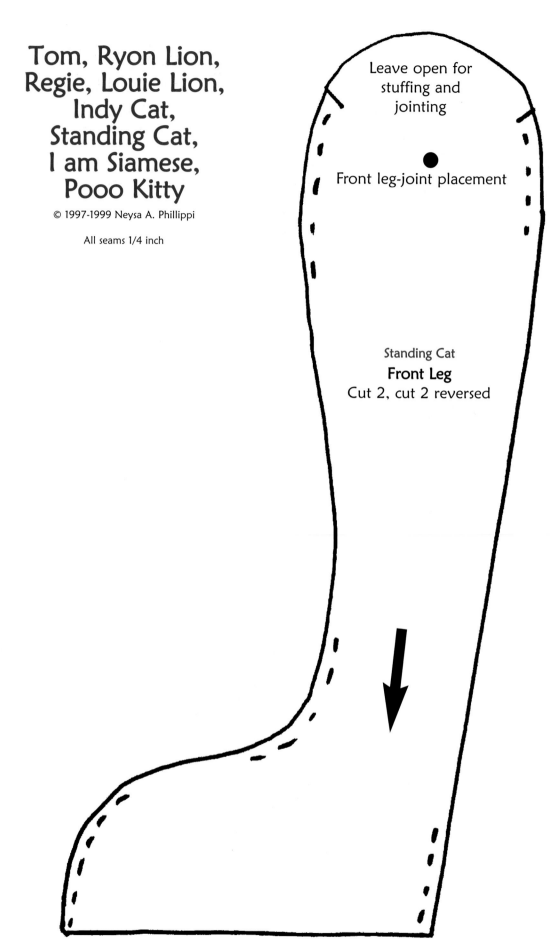

Leave open for stuffing and jointing

● Front leg-joint placement

Standing Cat
Front Leg
Cut 2, cut 2 reversed

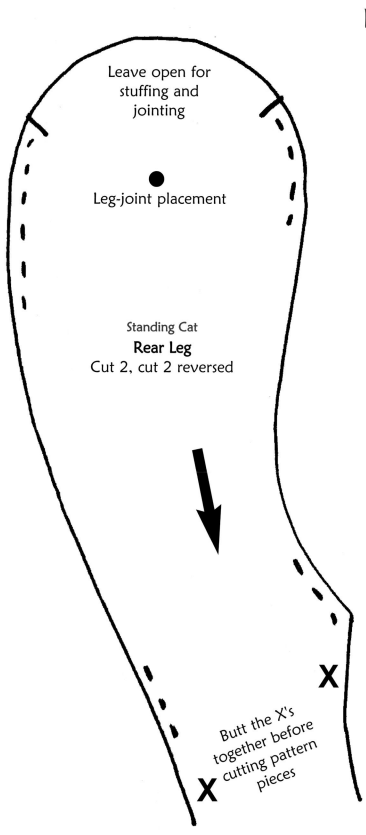

Leave open for
stuffing and
jointing

Leg-joint placement

Standing Cat
Rear Leg
Cut 2, cut 2 reversed

X

X

Butt the X's
together before
cutting pattern
pieces

Tom, Ryon Lion,
Regie, Louie Lion,
Indy Cat,
Standing Cat,
I am Siamese,
Pooo Kitty

© 1997-1999 Neysa A. Phillippi

All seams 1/4 inch

Tom, Ryon Lion, Regie, Louie Lion, Indy Cat, Standing Cat, I am Siamese, Pooo Kitty

All seams 1/4 inch

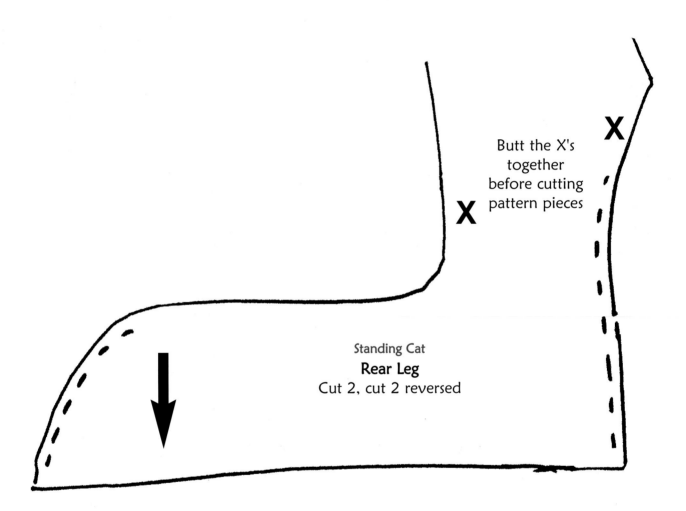

Butt the X's together before cutting pattern pieces

X

X

Standing Cat
Rear Leg
Cut 2, cut 2 reversed

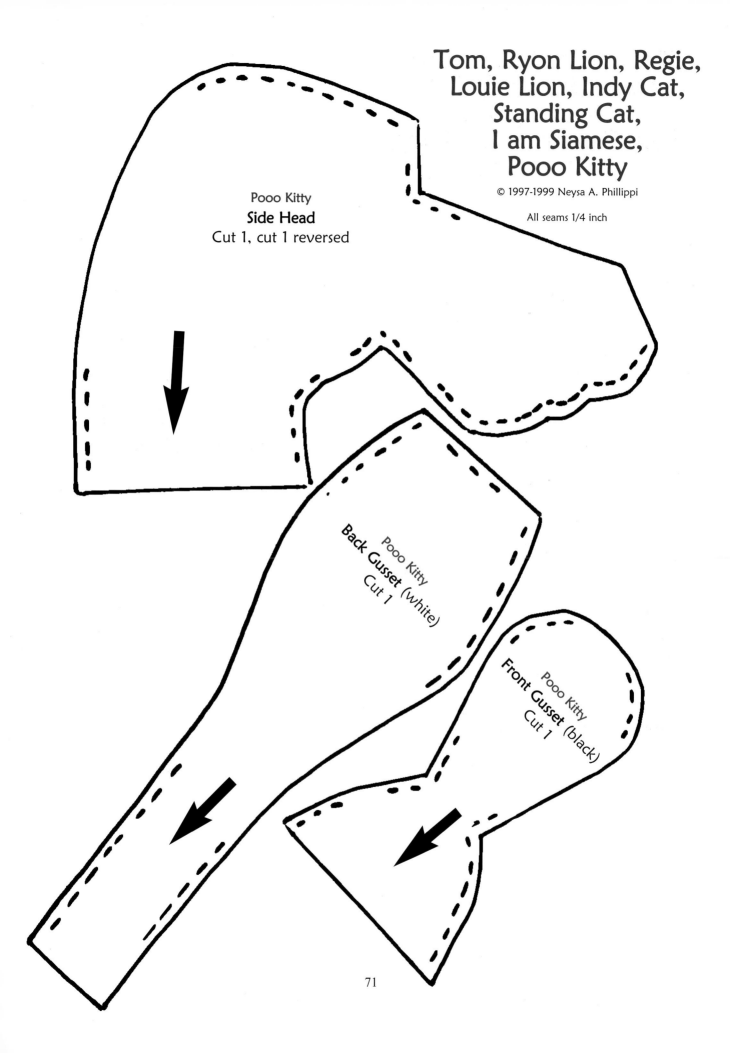

Tom, Ryon Lion, Regie,
Louie Lion, Indy Cat,
Standing Cat,
I am Siamese,
Pooo Kitty

© 1997-1999 Neysa A. Phillippi

All seams 1/4 inch

Pooo Kitty
Side Head
Cut 1, cut 1 reversed

Pooo Kitty
Back Gusset (white)
Cut 1

Pooo Kitty
Front Gusset (black)
Cut 1

71

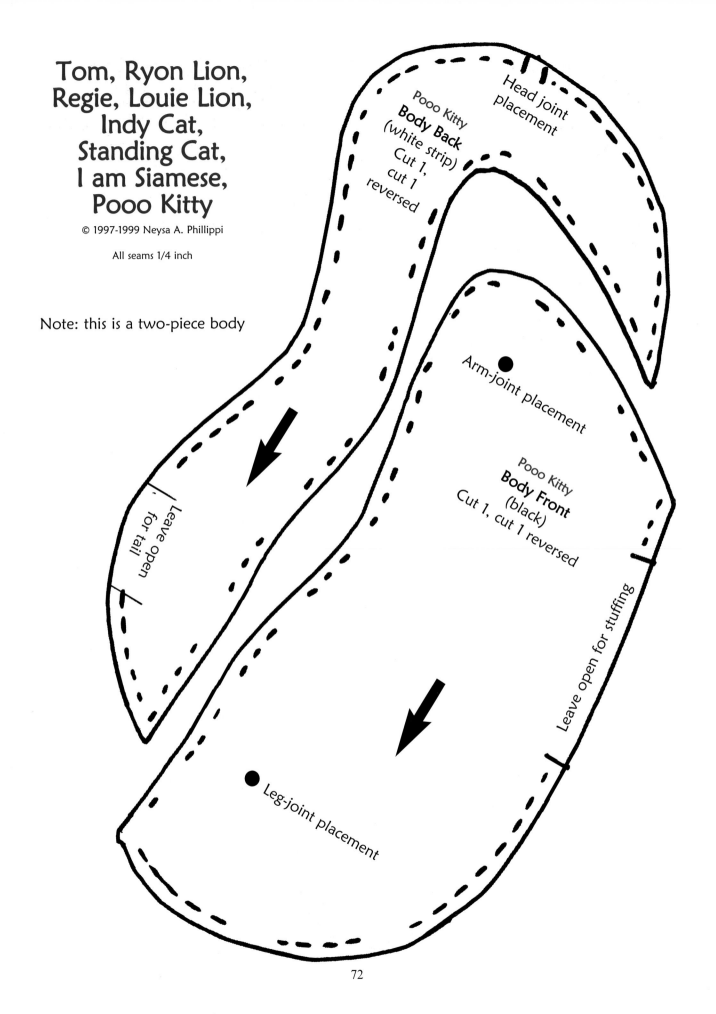

Tom, Ryon Lion,
Regie, Louie Lion,
Indy Cat,
Standing Cat,
I am Siamese,
Pooo Kitty

© 1997-1999 Neysa A. Phillippi

All seams 1/4 inch

Note: this is a two-piece body

Pooo Kitty
Body Back
(white strip)
Cut 1,
cut 1
reversed

Head joint
placement

Arm-joint placement

Pooo Kitty
Body Front
(black)
Cut 1, cut 1 reversed

Leave open for stuffing

Leave open for tail

Leg-joint placement

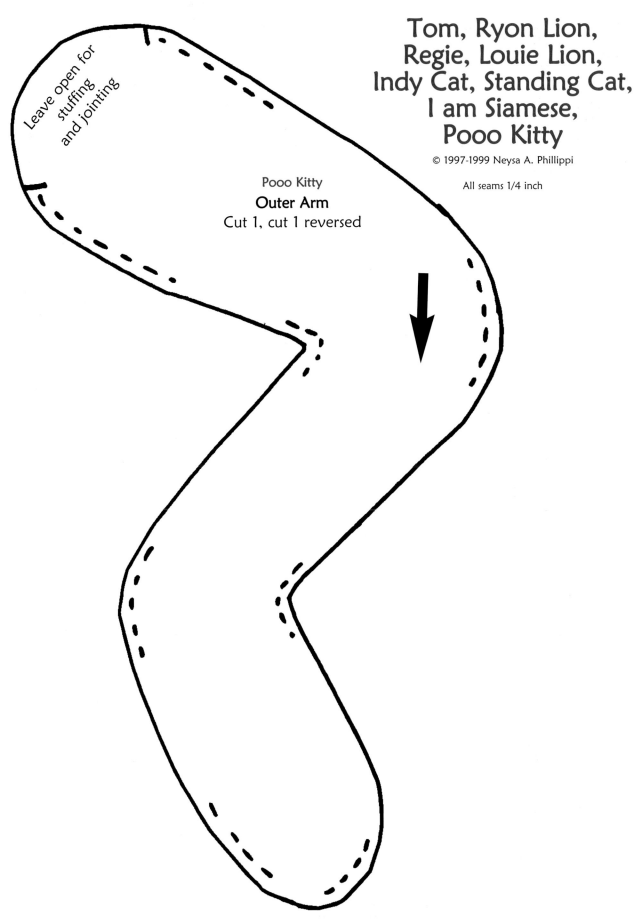

Leave open for stuffing and jointing

Tom, Ryon Lion,
Regie, Louie Lion,
Indy Cat, Standing Cat,
I am Siamese,
Pooo Kitty

© 1997-1999 Neysa A. Phillippi

All seams 1/4 inch

Pooo Kitty
Outer Arm
Cut 1, cut 1 reversed

73

Tom, Ryon Lion, Regie, Louie Lion, Indy Cat, Standing Cat, I am Siamese, Pooo Kitty

All seams 1/4 inch

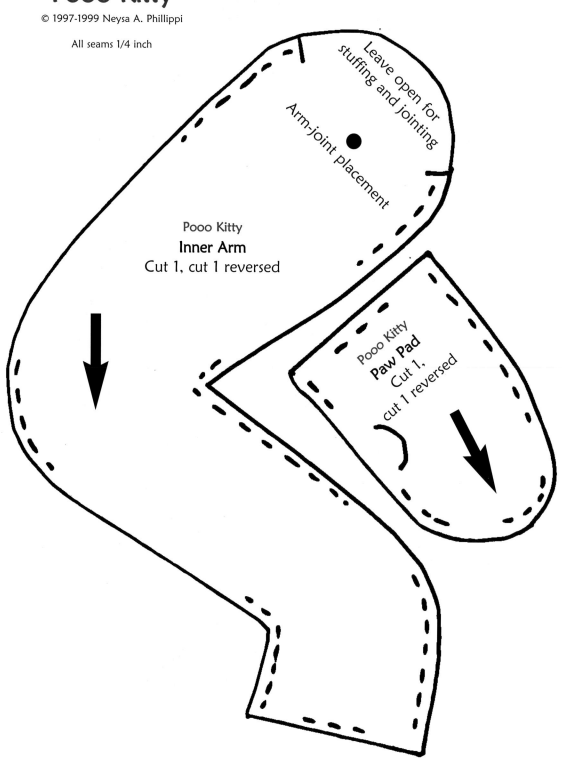

Leave open for stuffing and jointing

Arm-joint placement

Pooo Kitty
Inner Arm
Cut 1, cut 1 reversed

Pooo Kitty
Paw Pad
Cut 1,
cut 1 reversed

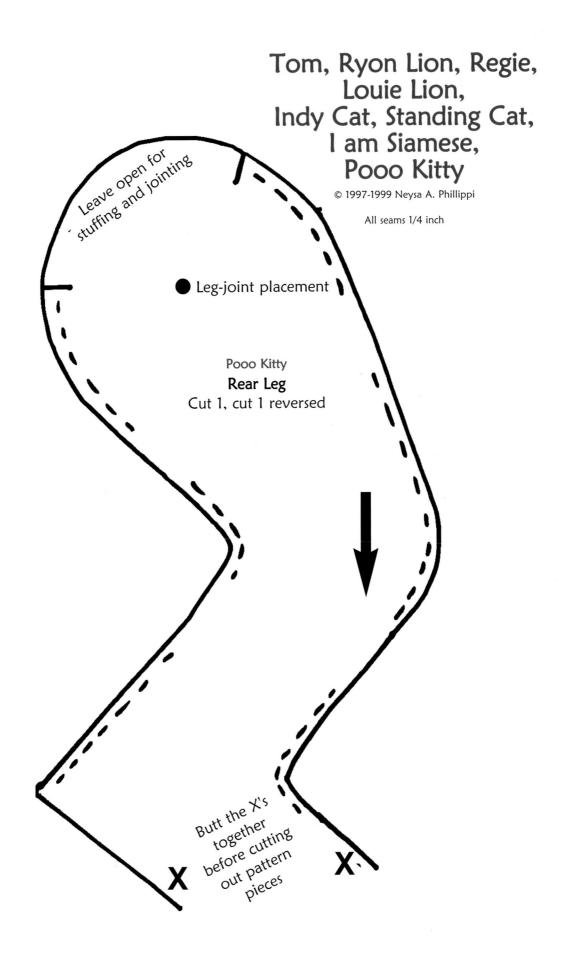

Tom, Ryon Lion, Regie,
Louie Lion,
Indy Cat, Standing Cat,
I am Siamese,
Pooo Kitty

© 1997-1999 Neysa A. Phillippi

All seams 1/4 inch

Leave open for stuffing and jointing

● Leg-joint placement

Pooo Kitty
Rear Leg
Cut 1, cut 1 reversed

Butt the X's together before cutting out pattern pieces

X   X

Tom, Ryon Lion, Regie, Louie Lion, Indy Cat, Standing Cat, I am Siamese, Pooo Kitty

All seams 1/4 inch

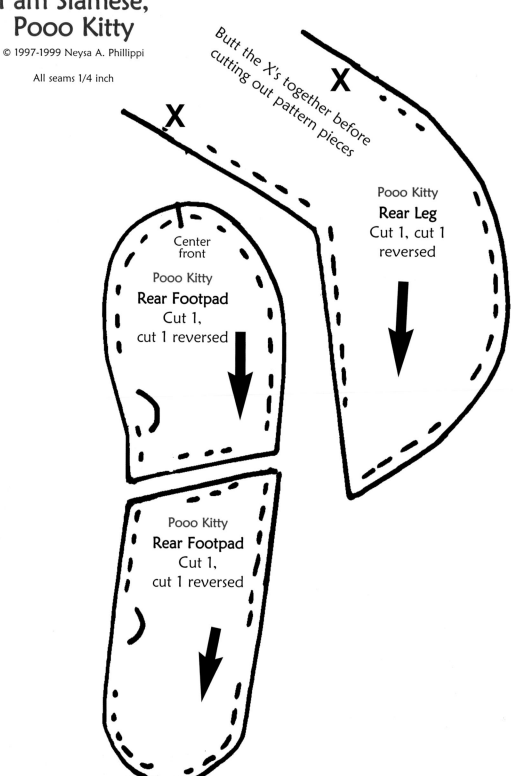

Butt the X's together before cutting out pattern pieces

X

X

Center front

Pooo Kitty
Rear Footpad
Cut 1,
cut 1 reversed

Pooo Kitty
Rear Leg
Cut 1, cut 1
reversed

Pooo Kitty
Rear Footpad
Cut 1,
cut 1 reversed

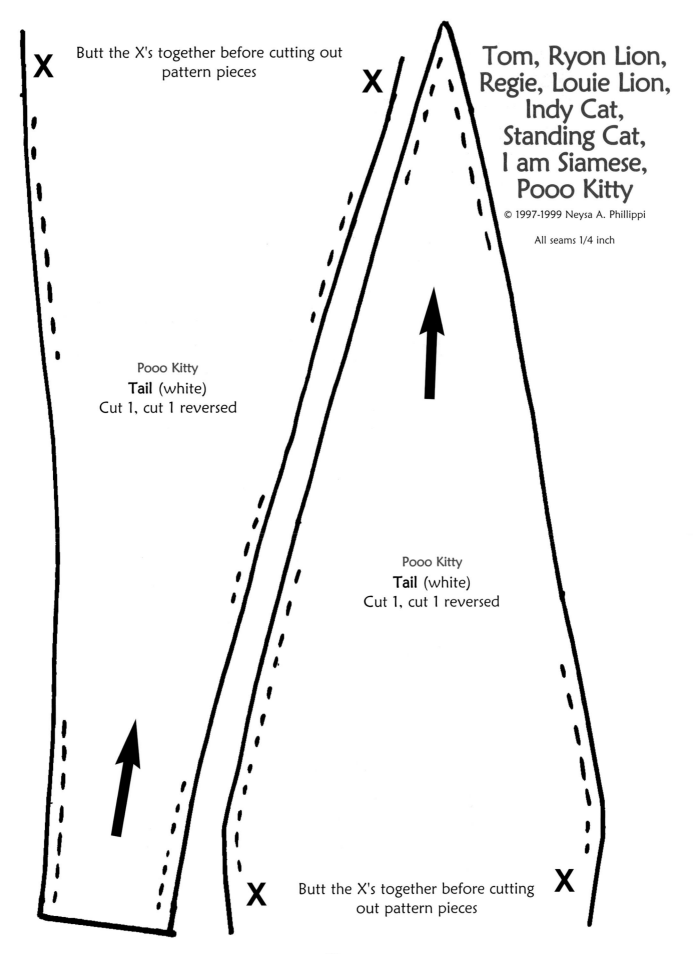

Butt the X's together before cutting out pattern pieces

X

Tom, Ryon Lion,
Regie, Louie Lion,
Indy Cat,
Standing Cat,
I am Siamese,
Pooo Kitty

© 1997-1999 Neysa A. Phillippi

All seams 1/4 inch

Pooo Kitty
Tail (white)
Cut 1, cut 1 reversed

Pooo Kitty
Tail (white)
Cut 1, cut 1 reversed

Butt the X's together before cutting out pattern pieces

77

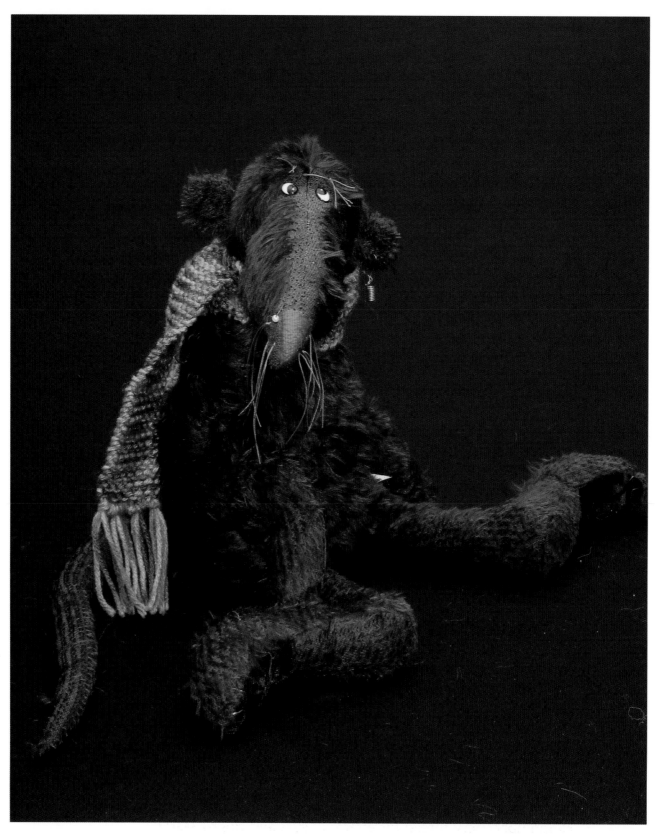

Dudley the Rat is from my *City Rat Series*, in which rats are as big as cats. He has bent arms and straight legs. He is nineteen inches (48 cm) tall and has a seventeen-inch-long (43 cm) tail. Dudley is a follower; he's not the brightest rat on the block, but you have to love him anyway. To make a smaller version of Dudley, copy the original pattern at fifty-five percent.

Dudley the Rat

Dudley the Rat is fully jointed; he's nineteen inches (48 cm) tall and has a seventeen-inch-long (43 cm) tail.

To make the smaller version of Dudley, which is featured below, make a copy at fifty-five percent of the original pattern size. The finished rat from the reduced pattern will be ten inches (25 cm) tall.

Materials

- 1/2 yard (18 x 54 inches or 30 x 36 inches) mohair, any style, color and length desired (1/4 yard if you are making the smaller version)

- 9-inch-square of velour upholstery fabric, felt, ultra suede or other fabric for paw pads

- One pair of 4-mm glass or plastic eyes (larger eyes are okay, if preferred)

- Three sets of 35-mm joints for head and arms and two sets of 45-mm joints for legs (if you are making the smaller version, you need five sets of 20-mm joints)

- Yarn for nose and mouth

- Sewing machine thread for seams to match mohair color (if stuffing with pellets, sew all seams twice)

- Nylon upholstery thread for attaching eyes and closing seams

- Polyester stuffing and plastic pellets

Dudley the Rat

54 inches

18 inches

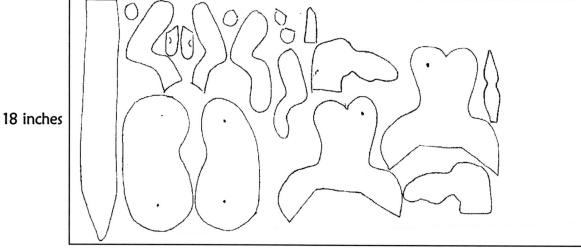

1/2 yard (30 x 36 inches or 18 x 54 inches) needed

9-inch-square velour, felt or other fabric needed for the paw and foot pads

9 inches

9 inches

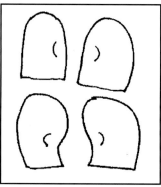

Directions

Read and follow the basic directions for layout, cutting, pinning and sewing.

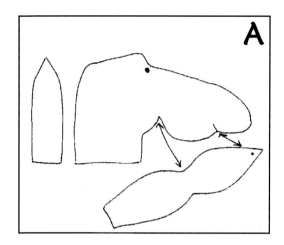

Head: Sew side head and neck gusset as shown in **Diagram A**, matching points and easing in the neck gusset to fit the underside of the side head. Sew both side heads to the neck gusset, and then sew the back head gusset to the side heads. Lastly, sew the side head to the side head, making a center-seam head.

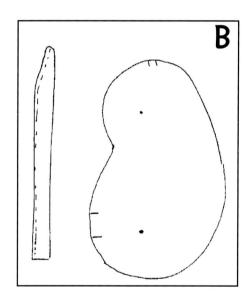

Body and Tail: Before you sew the body, fold the tail in half as shown in **Diagram B**. Pin and sew the tail, leaving one end open. Turn right side out. Loosely stuff the tail; I suggest using plastic pellets for this. Once it is stuffed, sew the tail's end closed. Insert the tail between the two body pieces (i.e., sandwiched between the two right sides of the body). Pin in place. Sew the body together. Turn body right side out.

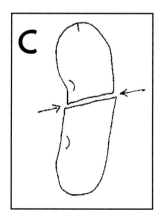

Foot Pads: Dudley has a two-piece foot pad, as shown in **Diagram C**. Sew the two pieces together at arrows; sew the pad to the legs as previously instructed.

To create a floppy rat, loosely stuff and joint Dudley.

Dudley the Rat

© 1999 Neysa A. Phillippi

All seams 1/4 inch

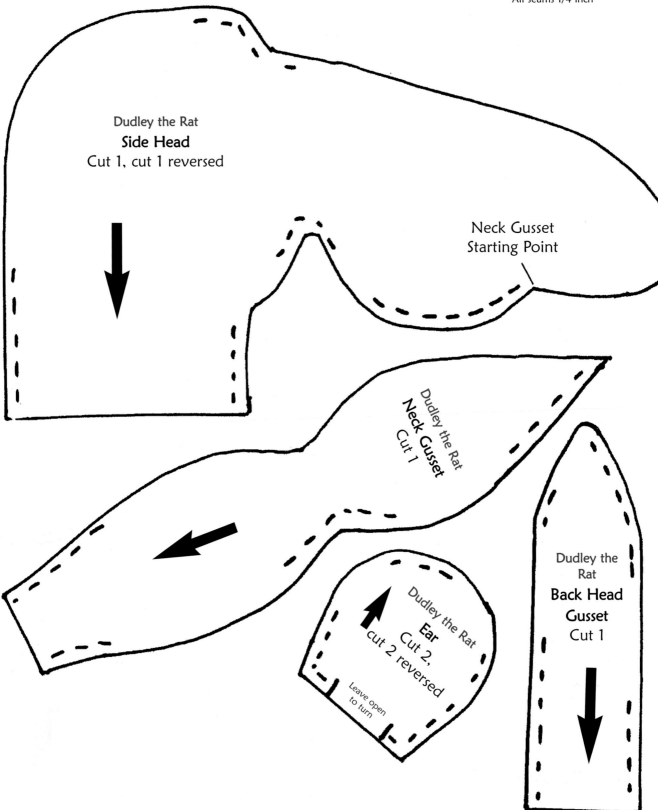

Dudley the Rat
Side Head
Cut 1, cut 1 reversed

Neck Gusset
Starting Point

Dudley the Rat
Neck Gusset
Cut 1

Dudley the
Rat
**Back Head
Gusset**
Cut 1

Dudley the Rat
Ear
Cut 2,
cut 2 reversed

Leave open
to turn

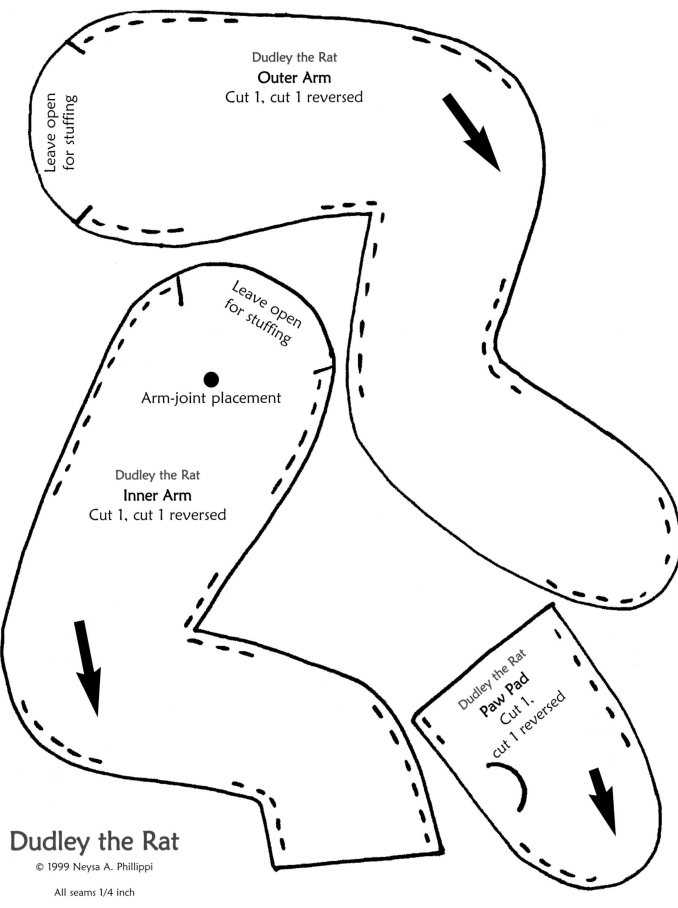

Dudley the Rat
Outer Arm
Cut 1, cut 1 reversed

Leave open for stuffing

Leave open for stuffing

Arm-joint placement

Dudley the Rat
Inner Arm
Cut 1, cut 1 reversed

Dudley the Rat
Paw Pad
Cut 1,
cut 1 reversed

Dudley the Rat

© 1999 Neysa A. Phillippi

All seams 1/4 inch

Dudley the Rat

All seams 1/4 inch

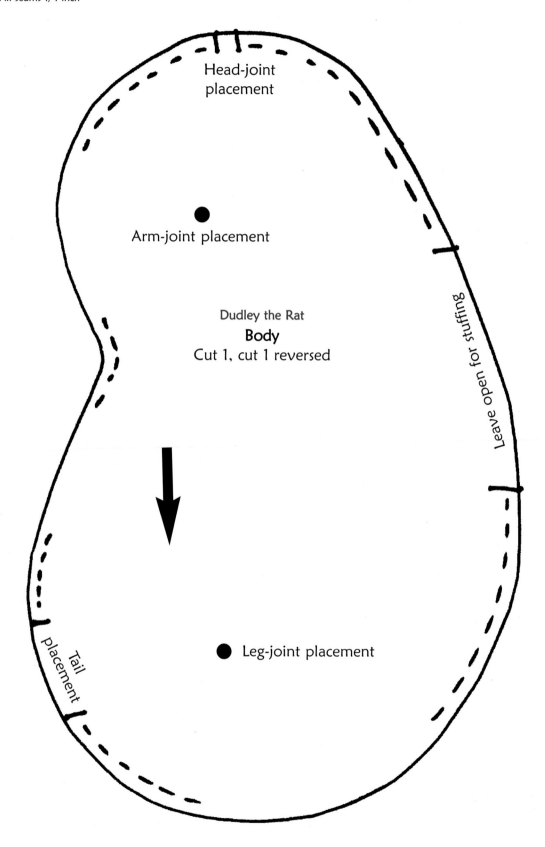

Head-joint placement

Arm-joint placement

Dudley the Rat
Body
Cut 1, cut 1 reversed

Leave open for stuffing

Tail placement

Leg-joint placement

Dudley the Rat

All seams 1/4 inch

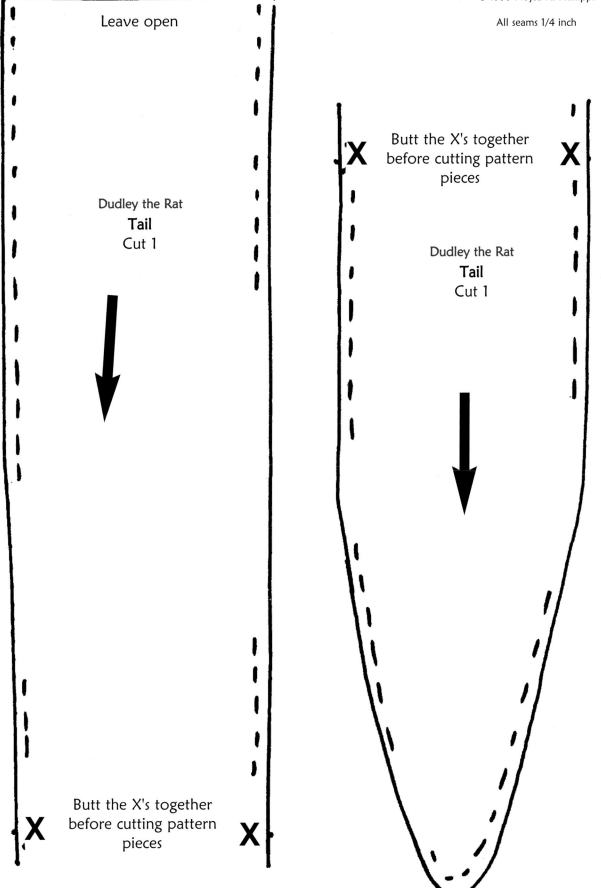

Leave open

Dudley the Rat
Tail
Cut 1

Butt the X's together
before cutting pattern
pieces

X   X

Butt the X's together
before cutting pattern
pieces

X   X

Dudley the Rat
Tail
Cut 1

Dudley the Rat

© 1999 Neysa A. Phillippi

All seams 1/4 inch

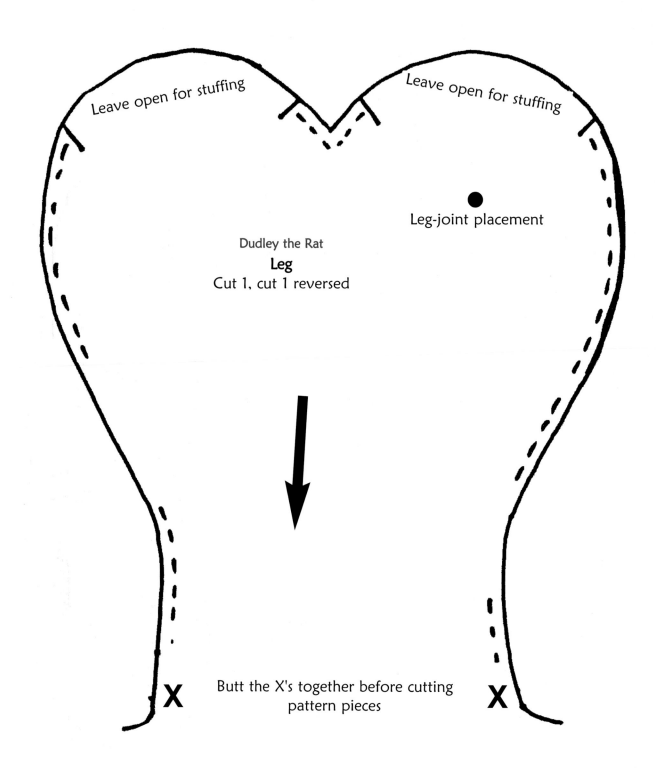

Leave open for stuffing

Leave open for stuffing

Leg-joint placement

Dudley the Rat

Leg
Cut 1, cut 1 reversed

X

X

Butt the X's together before cutting
pattern pieces

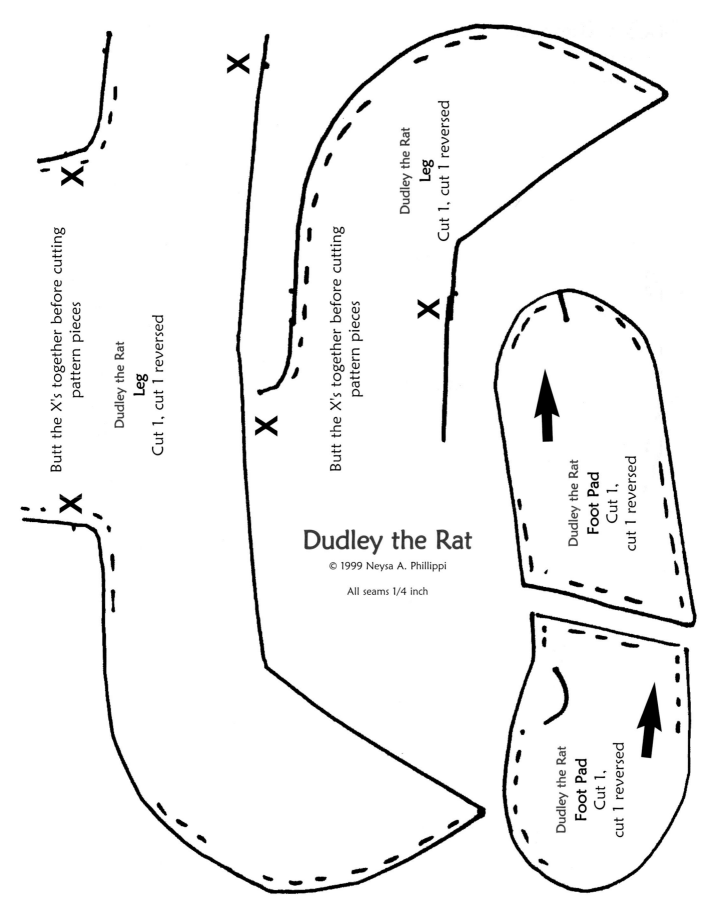

Butt the X's together before cutting
pattern pieces

Dudley the Rat
Leg
Cut 1, cut 1 reversed

Butt the X's together before cutting
pattern pieces

Dudley the Rat
Leg
Cut 1, cut 1 reversed

Dudley the Rat
Leg
Cut 1, cut 1 reversed

Dudley the Rat

© 1999 Neysa A. Phillippi

All seams 1/4 inch

Dudley the Rat
Foot Pad
Cut 1,
cut 1 reversed

Dudley the Rat
Foot Pad
Cut 1,
cut 1 reversed

87

Rodney the Rat, from my *City Rat Series*, has bent arms and legs. He is the leader of his pack. Rodney is nineteen inches (48 cm) tall and has a sixteen-inch-long (40 cm) tail. Give him a scarf, and pierce his ears, nose and belly button if you want a funky rat friend.

Rodney the Rat

Rodney the Rat is fully jointed; he is nineteen inches (48 cm) tall and has a sixteen-inch long (40 cm) tail.

Materials

- 1/2 yard (18 x 54 inches or 30 x 36 inches) of mohair in any style, color and length

- 9-inch-square of velour upholstery fabric, felt, ultra suede or other fabric for paw pads

- One pair of 4-mm glass or plastic eyes; larger sizes are okay

- Three sets of 35-mm joints for the head and arms; two sets of 45-mm for the legs

- Yarn for the nose and mouth

- Sewing machine thread for seams to match mohair color (if stuffing with pellets, sew all seams twice)

- Nylon upholstery thread for attaching eyes and closing seams

- Polyester stuffing and plastic pellets

Rodney the Rat

54 inches

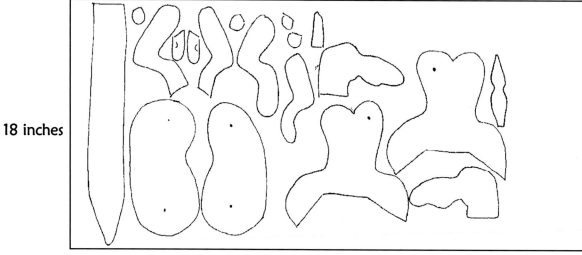

18 inches

1/2 yard (30 x 36 inches or 18 x 54 inches) fabric needed

9-inch-square
velour, felt or other
fabric needed for
the paw and foot
pads

9 inches

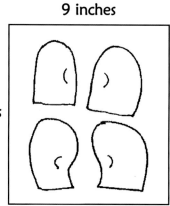

9 inches

Directions

Read and follow the basic directions for layout, cutting, pinning and sewing.

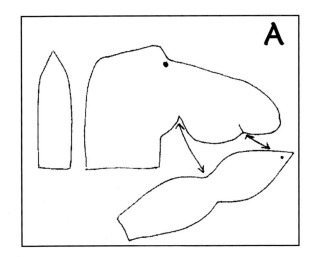

Head: Sew one side head and neck gusset as shown in **Diagram A**, matching the points and easing in neck gusset to fit the underside of side head. Sew the other side head to the neck gusset. Next, sew the back head gusset to the side heads. Sew the two side head pieces together, making a center-seam head.

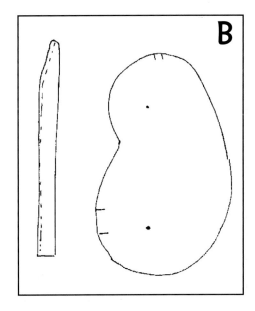

Body and Tail: Before you sew the body, fold the tail in half as shown in **Diagram B**. Pin and sew the tail, leaving one end open. Turn right side out. Loosely stuff the tail; I suggest using plastic pellets. Sew the end closed after stuffing. Insert the tail between the two body pieces and pin it in place. Sew the body together and turn it right side out.

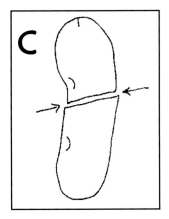

Foot Pads: Rodney's foot pad comes in two pieces, as shown in **Diagram C**. Sew the two together at the arrows, and then sew the pads to the leg in the normal manner.

To create a floppy rat, loosely stuff and joint Rodney.

91

Rodney the Rat

© 1998 Neysa A. Phillippi

All seams 1/4 inch

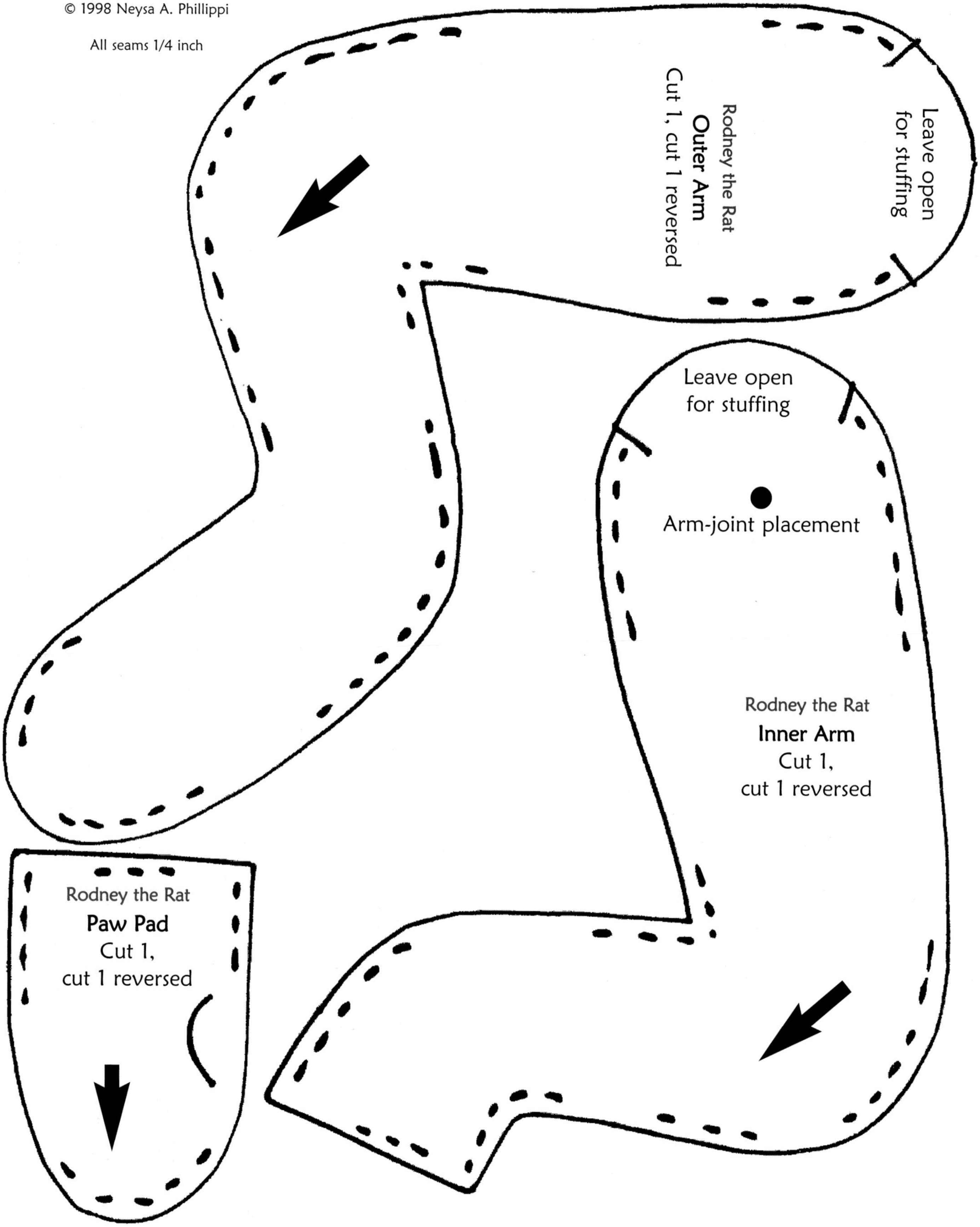

Leave open
for stuffing

Rodney the Rat
Outer Arm
Cut 1, cut 1 reversed

Leave open
for stuffing

• Arm-joint placement

Rodney the Rat
Inner Arm
Cut 1,
cut 1 reversed

Rodney the Rat
Paw Pad
Cut 1,
cut 1 reversed

Rodney the Rat

© 1998 Neysa A. Phillippi

All seams 1/4 inch

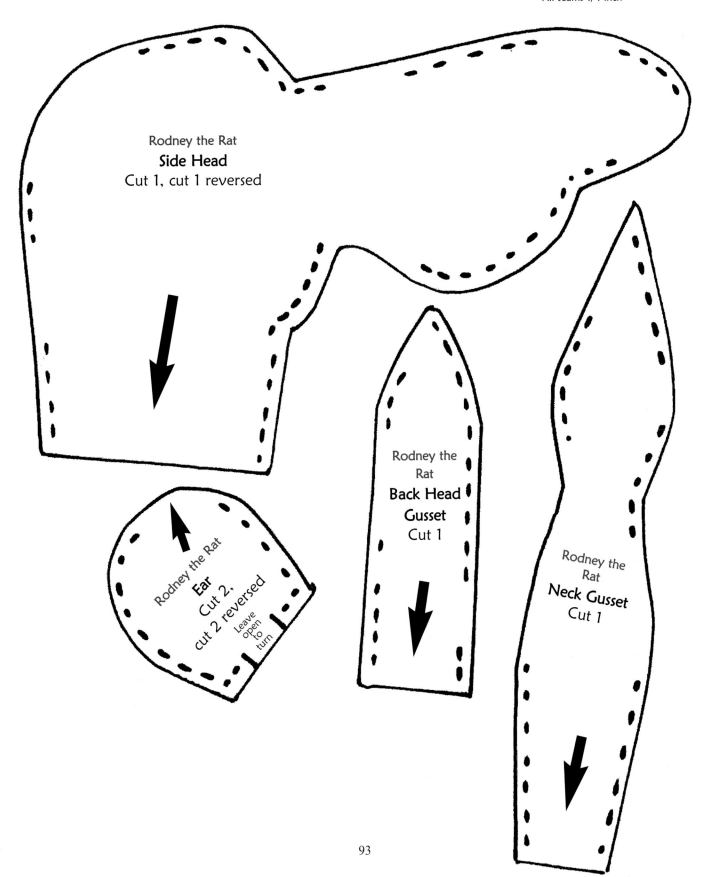

Rodney the Rat
Side Head
Cut 1, cut 1 reversed

Rodney the Rat
Ear
Cut 2,
cut 2 reversed
Leave open to turn

Rodney the Rat
Back Head Gusset
Cut 1

Rodney the Rat
Neck Gusset
Cut 1

93

Rodney the Rat

© 1998 Neysa A. Phillippi

All seams 1/4 inch

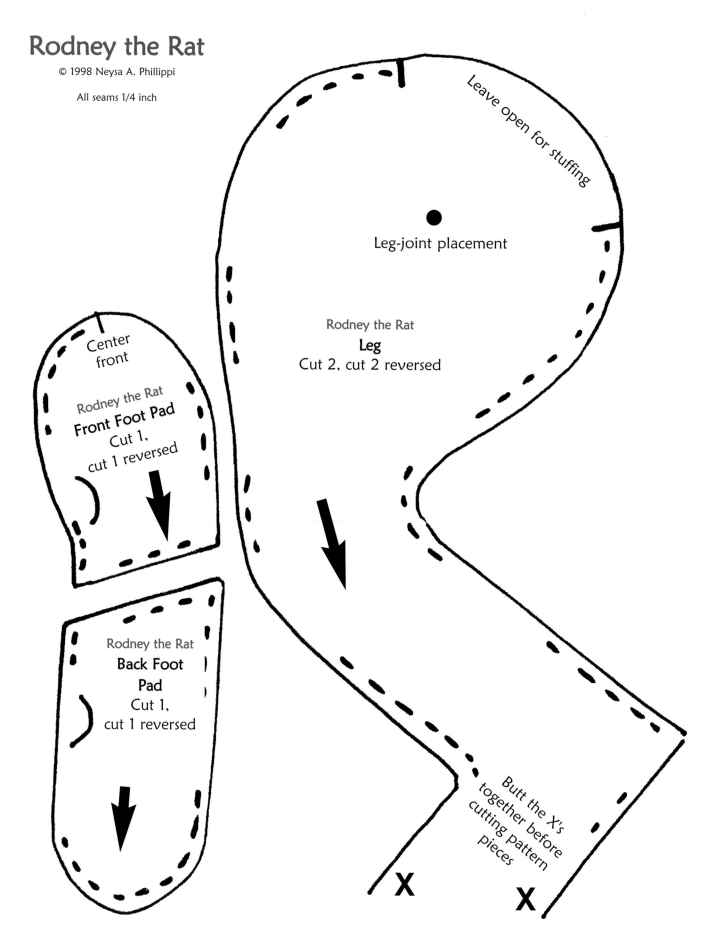

Leave open for stuffing

Leg-joint placement

Rodney the Rat
Leg
Cut 2, cut 2 reversed

Center front

Rodney the Rat
Front Foot Pad
Cut 1,
cut 1 reversed

Rodney the Rat
Back Foot Pad
Cut 1,
cut 1 reversed

Butt the X's together before cutting pattern pieces

X   X

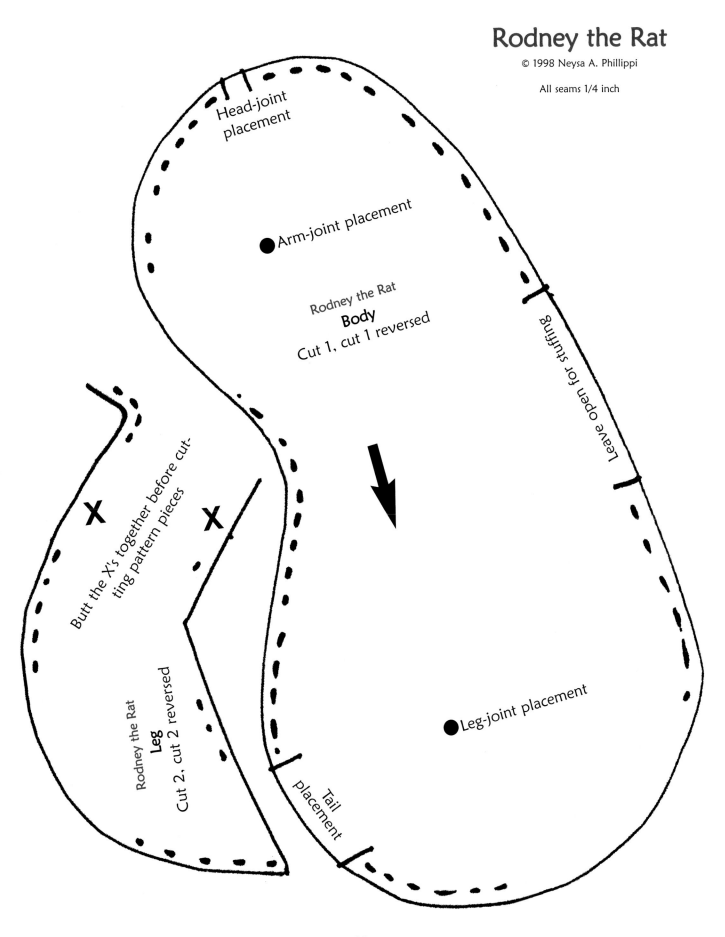

Rodney the Rat

© 1998 Neysa A. Phillippi

All seams 1/4 inch

Head-joint placement

Arm-joint placement

Rodney the Rat
Body
Cut 1, cut 1 reversed

Leave open for stuffing

Butt the X's together before cutting pattern pieces

Rodney the Rat
Leg
Cut 2, cut 2 reversed

Leg-joint placement

Tail placement

95

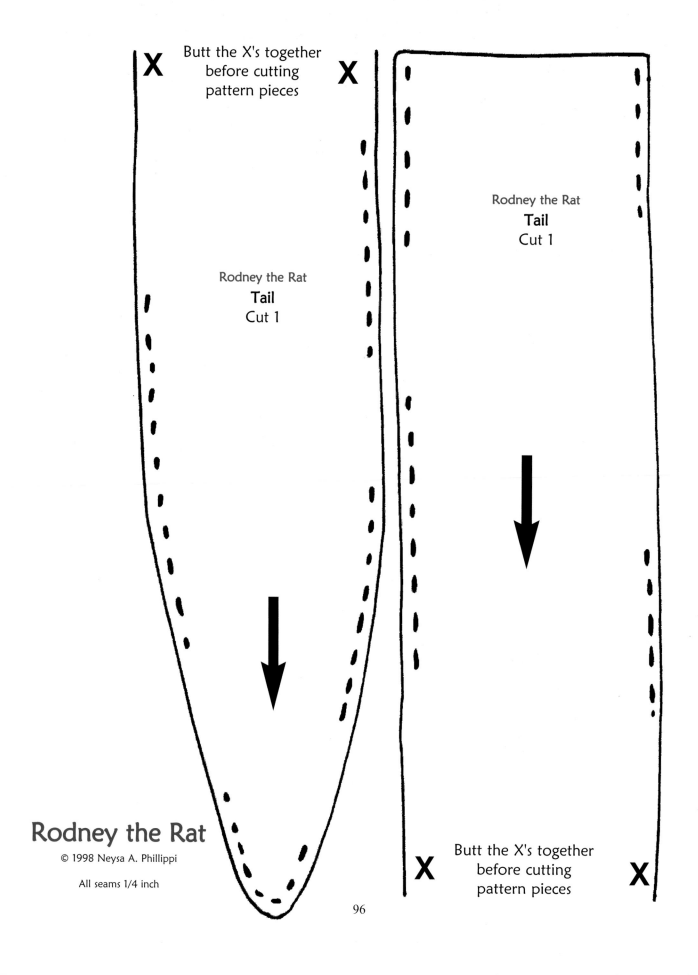

X Butt the X's together
before cutting
pattern pieces X

X Butt the X's together
before cutting
pattern pieces X

Rodney the Rat
Tail
Cut 1

Rodney the Rat
Tail
Cut 1

Rodney the Rat

© 1998 Neysa A. Phillippi

All seams 1/4 inch

96

U. Dirty
Rat

U. Dirty Rat, from my *City Rat Series*, has bent arms and straight legs, and is designed to lie down. He is twenty-six inches (66 cm) from his nose to his toes and has a sixteen-inch-long (40 cm) tail. The "gig" is up: An antique French rat trap has him by the tail!

U. Dirty Rat

U. Dirty Rat is fully jointed and twenty-six inches (66 cm) from his nose to his toes; he has a sixteen-inch-long (40 cm) tail.

Materials

- 1/2 yard (18 x 54 inches or 30 x 36 inches) mohair, in any style, color and length desired

- 9-inch-square of velour upholstery fabric, felt, ultra suede or other fabric for paw pads

- One pair of 4-mm glass or plastic eyes; larger sizes are okay

- Five sets of 35-mm joints

- Yarn for the nose and mouth

- Sewing machine thread for seams to match mohair color (if stuffing with pellets, sew all seams twice)

- Nylon upholstery thread for attaching the eyes and closing seams

- Polyester stuffing and plastic pellets

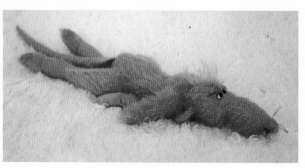

U. Dirty Rat

54 inches

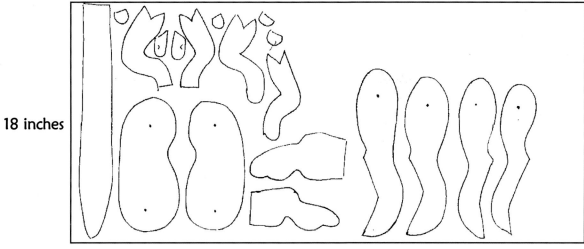

18 inches

1/2 yard (30 x 36 inches or 18 x 54 inches) needed

9-inch-square
velour, felt or other
fabric needed for
the paw and
foot pads

9 inches

9 inches

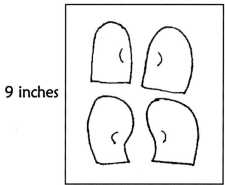

Directions

Read and follow the basic directions for layout, cutting, pinning and sewing.

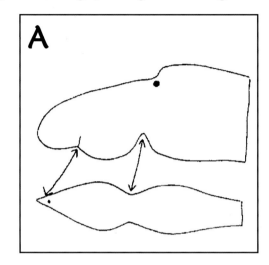

Head: Sew one side head and neck gusset as shown in **Diagram A**, matching points and easing the neck gusset in to fit the underside of the side head. Sew the other side head to the neck gusset. Now sew the side head pieces together, creating a center-seam head.

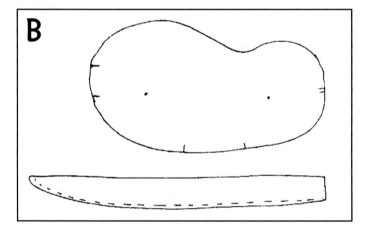

Body and Tail: Before you sew the body, fold the tail in half as shown in **Diagram B**. Pin and sew the tail, leaving one end open. Turn right side out. Loosely stuff the tail; I suggest using plastic pellets. Sew the end closed after stuffing. Insert the tail between the two body pieces and pin it in place. Sew the body together and turn it right side out.

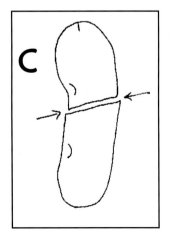

Arms: Follow the "Optional Arm" sewing directions included in the basic pattern directions (page 25).

Foot Pads: U. Dirty Rat's foot pad comes in two pieces, as shown in **Diagram C**. Sew the two together at the arrows, and then sew the foot pads to the legs in the usual manner.

To create a floppy rat, loosely stuff and joint U. Dirty Rat.

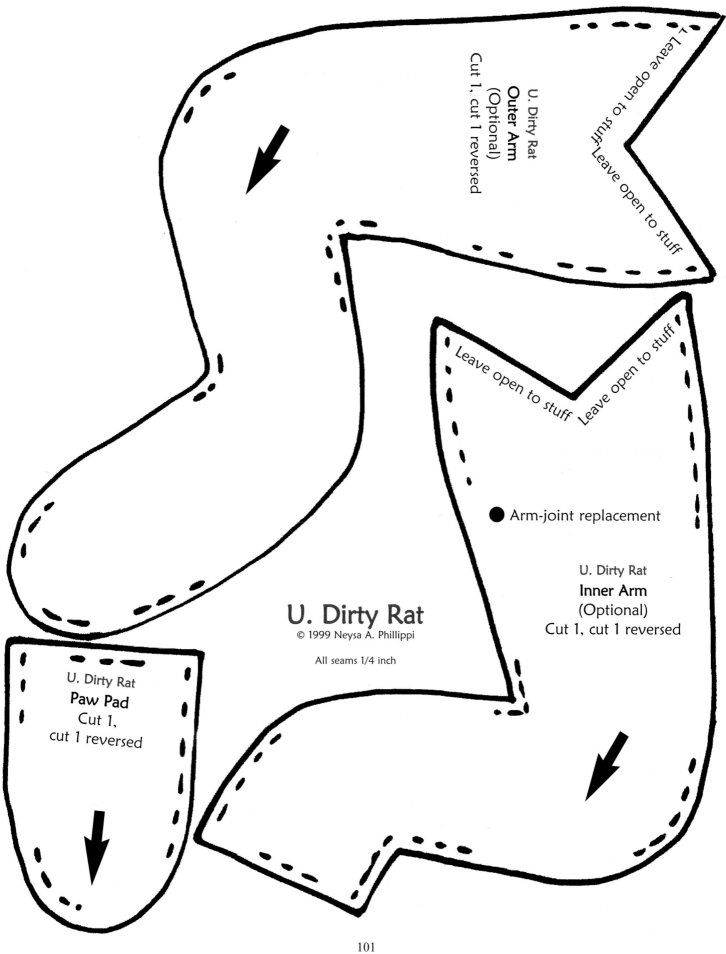

U. Dirty Rat
Outer Arm
(Optional)
Cut 1, cut 1 reversed

Leave open to stuff

Leave open to stuff

Leave open to stuff

Leave open to stuff

● Arm-joint replacement

U. Dirty Rat
Inner Arm
(Optional)
Cut 1, cut 1 reversed

U. Dirty Rat
© 1999 Neysa A. Phillippi

All seams 1/4 inch

U. Dirty Rat
Paw Pad
Cut 1,
cut 1 reversed

101

U. Dirty Rat

© 1999 Neysa A. Phillippi

All seams 1/4 inch

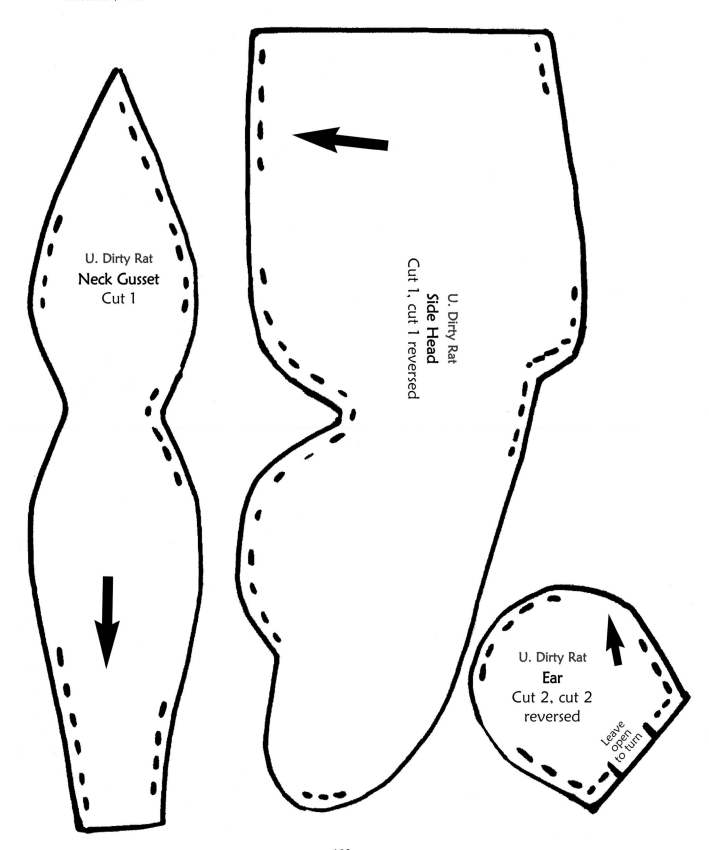

U. Dirty Rat
Neck Gusset
Cut 1

U. Dirty Rat
Side Head
Cut 1, cut 1 reversed

U. Dirty Rat
Ear
Cut 2, cut 2 reversed

Leave open to turn

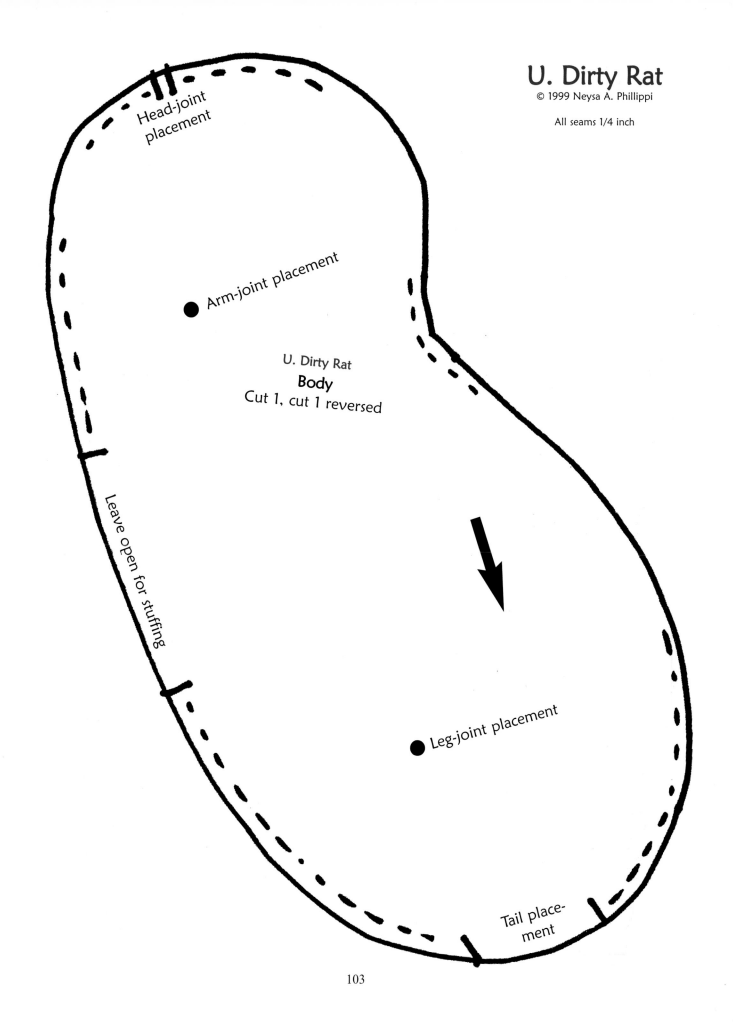

U. Dirty Rat
© 1999 Neysa A. Phillippi

All seams 1/4 inch

Head-joint placement

Arm-joint placement

U. Dirty Rat
Body
Cut 1, cut 1 reversed

Leave open for stuffing

Leg-joint placement

Tail placement

103

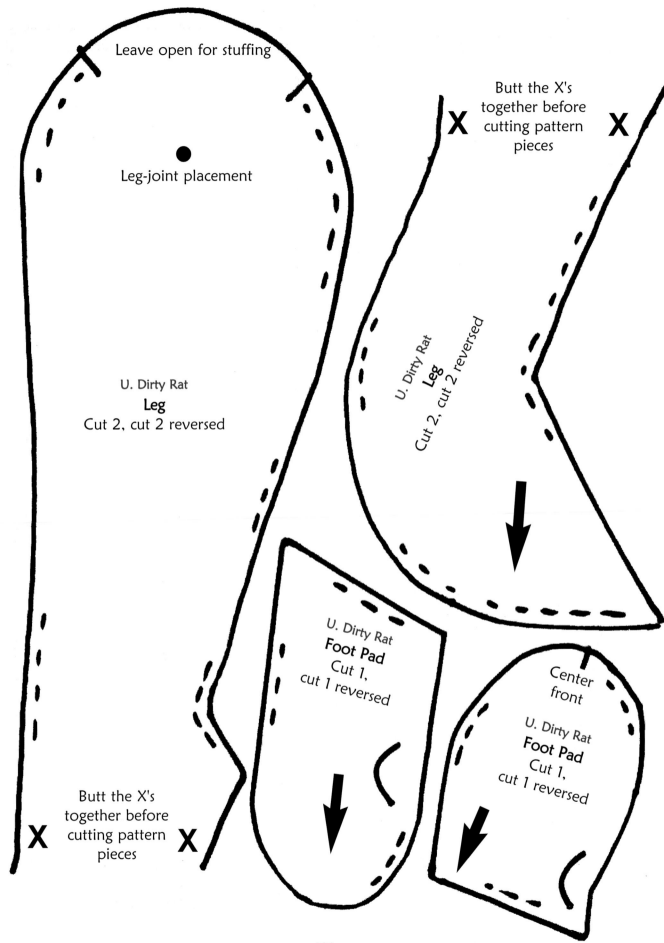

Leave open for stuffing

Leg-joint placement

U. Dirty Rat
Leg
Cut 2, cut 2 reversed

Butt the X's
together before
cutting pattern
pieces

X   X

U. Dirty Rat
Leg
Cut 2, cut 2 reversed

U. Dirty Rat
Foot Pad
Cut 1,
cut 1 reversed

Center
front

U. Dirty Rat
Foot Pad
Cut 1,
cut 1 reversed

Butt the X's
together before
cutting pattern
pieces

X   X

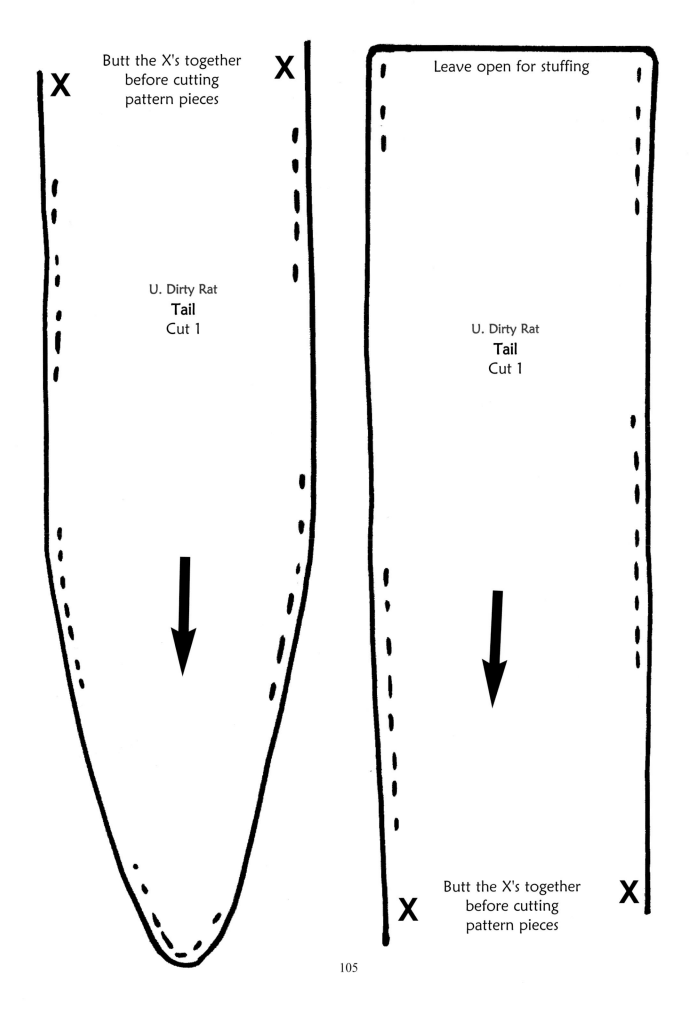

Butt the X's together
before cutting
pattern pieces

X

X

U. Dirty Rat
Tail
Cut 1

Leave open for stuffing

U. Dirty Rat
Tail
Cut 1

X

Butt the X's together
before cutting
pattern pieces

X

105

Chops is from my *BIG HEAD Series*; he is designed to recline, with his arms and legs extended as shown in the photographs on the opposite page. Chops is twenty inches (50 cm) from his nose to his toes and has a wired tail. You may also wire his ears, if desired.

Chops

Chops is fully jointed and twenty inches (50 cm) from his nose to his toes.

Materials

- 1/2 yard (18 x 54 inches or 30 x 36 inches) of mohair, any style, color and length desired

- 9-inch-square of velour upholstery fabric, felt, ultra suede or other fabric for paw pads

- One pair of 8-mm glass or plastic eyes

- Five sets of 35-mm joints

- Yarn for the nose

- Sewing machine thread for seams to match mohair color (if stuffing with pellets, sew all seams twice)

- Nylon upholstery thread for attaching the eyes and closing seams

- Floral wire or thin copper wire for the tail and ears (optional)

- Polyester stuffing and plastic pellets

Chops

54 inches

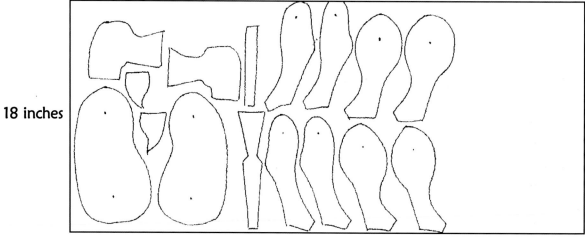

18 inches

1/2 yard (18 x 54 inches or 36 x 30 inches) of mohair needed

9-inch-square of velour, felt or other fabric for Front Paw Pads, Leg Paw Pads and Snout

9 inches

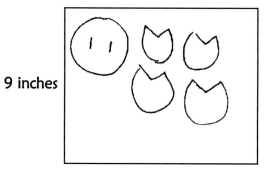

9 inches

Directions

Read and follow the basic directions for layout, cutting, pinning and sewing.

Head:
Sew the side head and neck gusset as you would a bear's head. The snout is sewn in place much as a paw pad is sewn to a leg. When sewing the snout, work carefully, checking to be sure that the fabric's nap is going down. After stuffing the head, stitch the nose yarn as illustrated on the snout pattern piece.

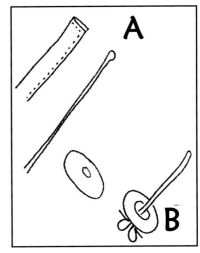

Ears:
Shave or trim the ears before sewing. Options: you can wire the pig's ears either by sewing thin floral wire between two seams or by tacking the wire to critical points on the ears, such as their tips and curves.

Body and Tail:
Before you sew the body, fold the tail as shown in **Diagram A**; pin and sew the tail, leaving one end open. Turn right side out. Cut a piece of floral or copper wire for the tail: it should be double the length of the tail, plus six inches. Fold the wire in half and insert it into the tail, leaving the extra wire exposed. Pin the wired tail between the two body pieces, once again leaving the excess wire exposed. Sew the pig's body together and turn right side out. Take a joint disk (at least a 35-mm disk) and place the exposed wire through the disk inside the body; turn the wire as you would a cotter pin, as shown in **Diagram B**. This anchors the tail firmly when the body is stuffed.

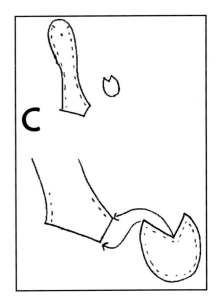

Arms and Legs:
The arms and legs are sewn together as shown in **Diagram C**. After sewing the arm and leg pieces together, pin and stitch the front and back leg paw pads to the arms and legs, noting that the paw pads for the legs are bigger than those for the arms (front legs). Placement is as shown in **Diagram C**. Pin and sew. Turn right side out.

When stuffed, the arms and legs should resemble those in the accompanying illustration.

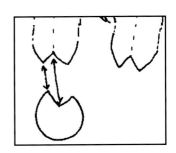

Stuff and joint as you would a bear. To make a floppy pig, stuff Chops loosely.

Chops

© 2000 Neysa A. Phillippi

All seams 1/4 inch

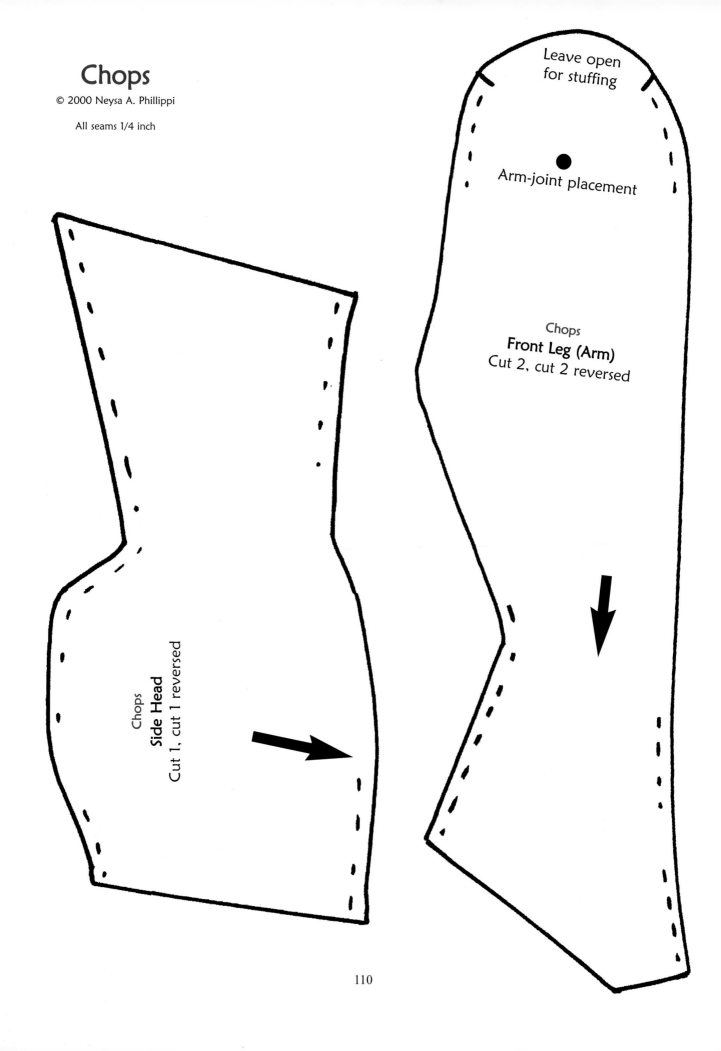

Leave open
for stuffing

● Arm-joint placement

Chops
Front Leg (Arm)
Cut 2, cut 2 reversed

Chops
Side Head
Cut 1, cut 1 reversed

110

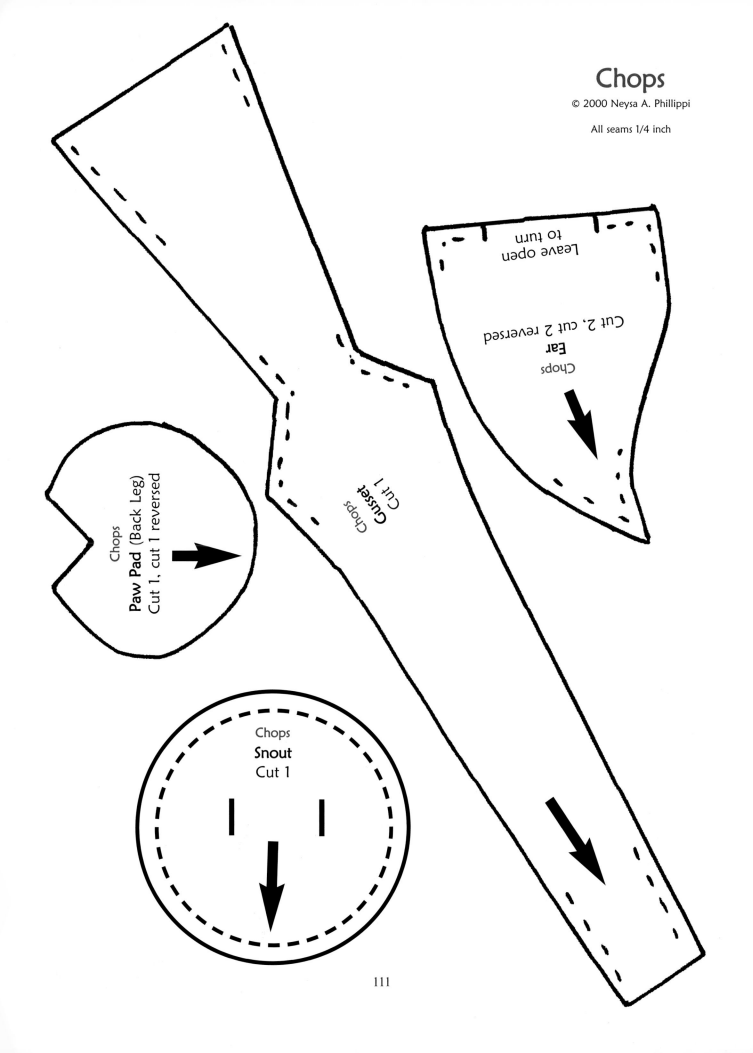

Chops

© 2000 Neysa A. Phillippi

All seams 1/4 inch

Leave open to turn

Chops
Ear
Cut 2, cut 2 reversed

Chops
Gusset
Cut 1

Chops
Paw Pad (Back Leg)
Cut 1, cut 1 reversed

Chops
Snout
Cut 1

Chops

© 2000 Neysa A. Phillippi

All seams 1/4 inch

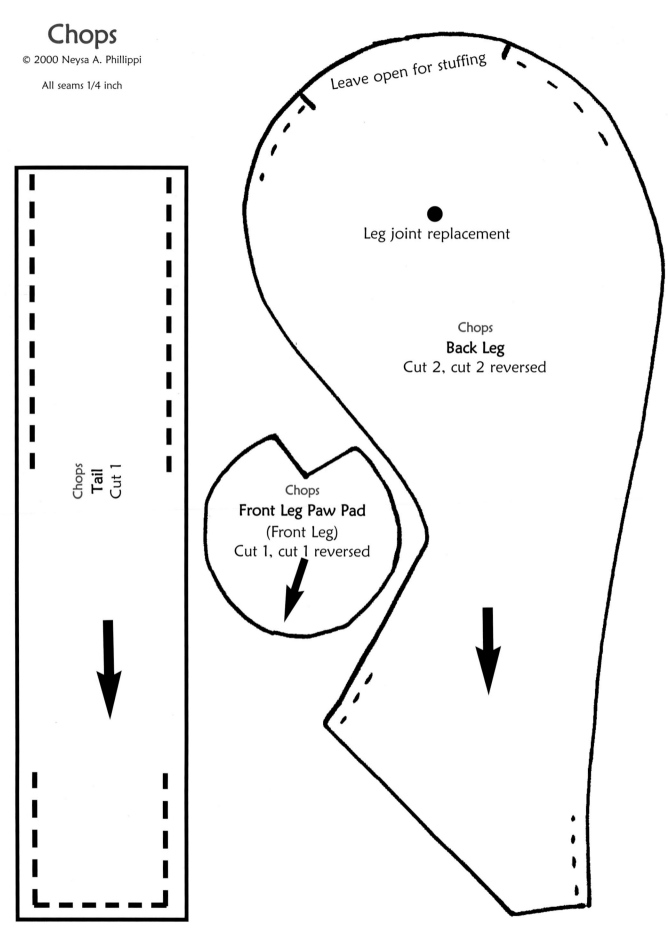

Leave open for stuffing

Leg joint replacement

Chops
Back Leg
Cut 2, cut 2 reversed

Chops
Front Leg Paw Pad
(Front Leg)
Cut 1, cut 1 reversed

Chops
Tail
Cut 1

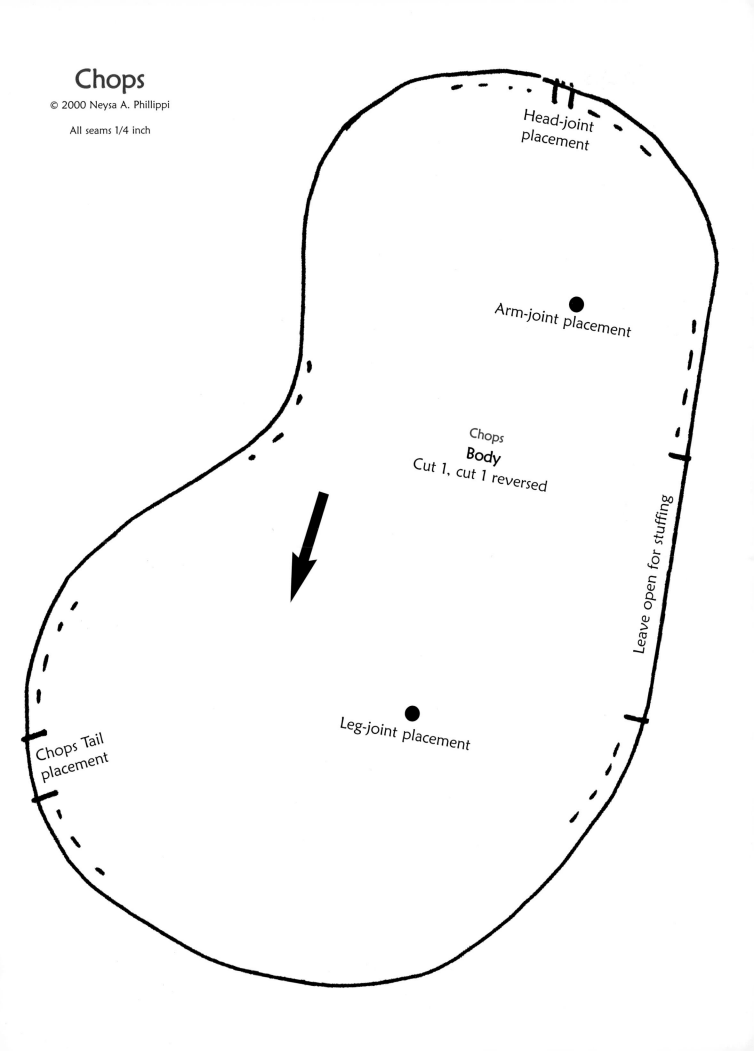

Chops

© 2000 Neysa A. Phillippi

All seams 1/4 inch

Head-joint
placement

Arm-joint placement

Chops
Body
Cut 1, cut 1 reversed

Leave open for stuffing

Leg-joint placement

Chops Tail
placement

Pig Floyd, from the *BIG HEAD Series*, is a very handsome pig. He's named for a very famous group and is designed to sit like a teddy bear. He is nineteen inches (48 cm) tall, and has wired ears and a wired tail.

Pig Floyd

Pig Floyd is fully jointed and nineteen inches (48 cm) tall.

Materials

- 1/2 yard of mohair (18 x 54 inches or 36 x 30 inches), any style, color and length
- 9-inch-square of velour upholstery fabric, felt, ultra suede or other fabric for paw pads
- One pair of 9-mm glass or plastic eyes
- Three sets of 35-mm joints for the head and arms; two sets of 45-mm joints for the legs
- Yarn for the nose
- Sewing machine thread for seams to match mohair color (if stuffing with pellets, sew all seams twice)
- Nylon upholstery thread for attaching eyes and closing seams
- Floral wire or thin copper wire for the tail and ears
- Polyester stuffing and plastic pellets

Pig Floyd

54 inches

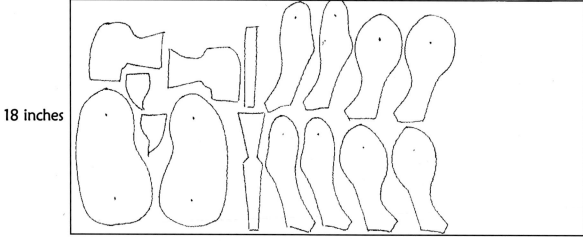

18 inches

1/2 yard (18 x 54 inches or 36 x 30 inches) needed

9-inch-square of velour, felt or other fabric for Front Paw Pads, Leg Paw Pads and Snout

9 inches

9 inches

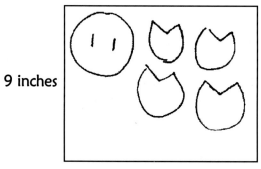

Directions

Read and follow basic directions for layout, cutting, pinning and sewing.

Head: Sew the two side head pieces to the gusset; the pig's snout is sewn to the head in the same way the paw pads are sewn to the arms and legs. When attaching the snout, be sure that the fabric's nap is going down. Stitch the nose yarn as illustrated on the snout pattern piece.

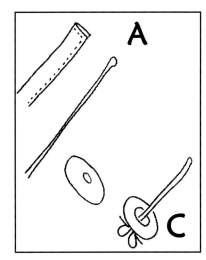

Ears: Shave or trim the ears before sewing. Wire the pig's ears either by sewing thin floral wire between the two seams or by tacking the wire to critical points on the ears, such as their tips and curves.

Body and Tail: Before you sew the body, fold the tail as shown in **Diagram A**, and then pin and sew its seams, leaving

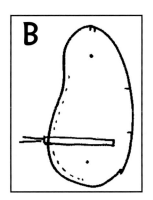

one end open. Turn right side out. Cut a piece of floral or copper wire for the tail: it should be double the length of the tail, plus six inches. Fold the wire in half and insert it into the tail, leaving the extra wire exposed. Pin the wired tail between the two body pieces as shown in **Diagram B**, leaving the excess wire exposed. Sew the pig's body. Turn body right side out. Take a joint disk (at least a 35-mm disk) and place the exposed wire through the disk inside the body; turn the wire as you would a cotter pin, as shown in **Diagram C**. This anchors the tail firmly when the body is stuffed.

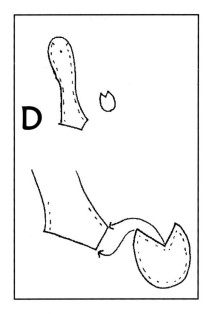

Arms and Legs: Sew the arms and legs together as shown in **Diagram D**. After sewing the arm and leg pieces together, pin and stitch the front and back leg paw pads to the arms and legs, noting that the legs' paw pads are bigger than the arms' pads. Placement is shown in **Diagram D**. Pin and sew; turn right side out.

When stuffed, the arms and legs should look like the illustration at right. Stuff and joint as you would a bear.

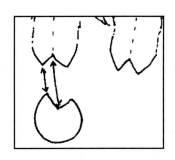

Pig Floyd

© 1999 Neysa A. Phillippi

All seams 1/4 inch

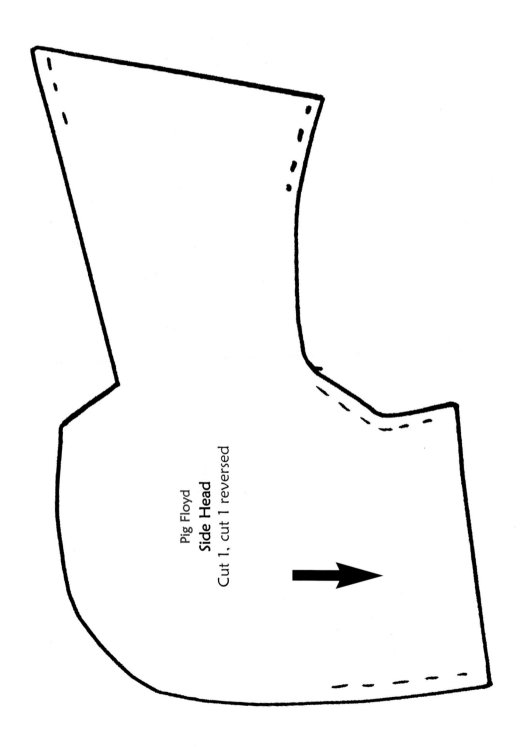

Pig Floyd
Side Head
Cut 1, cut 1 reversed

All seams 1/4 inch

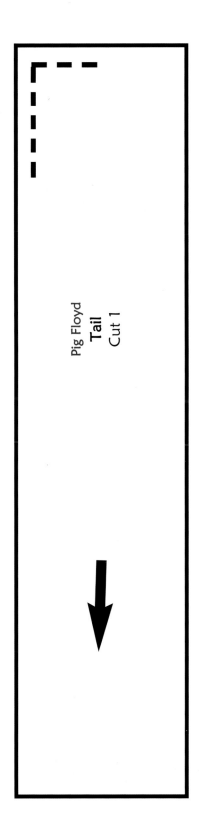

Pig Floyd
Tail
Cut 1

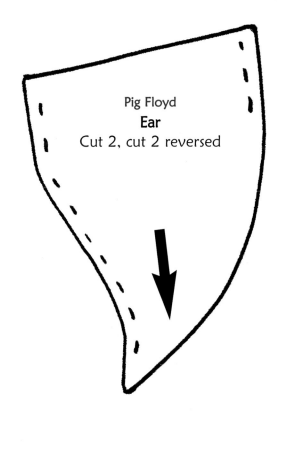

Pig Floyd
Ear
Cut 2, cut 2 reversed

Pig Floyd

All seams 1/4 inch

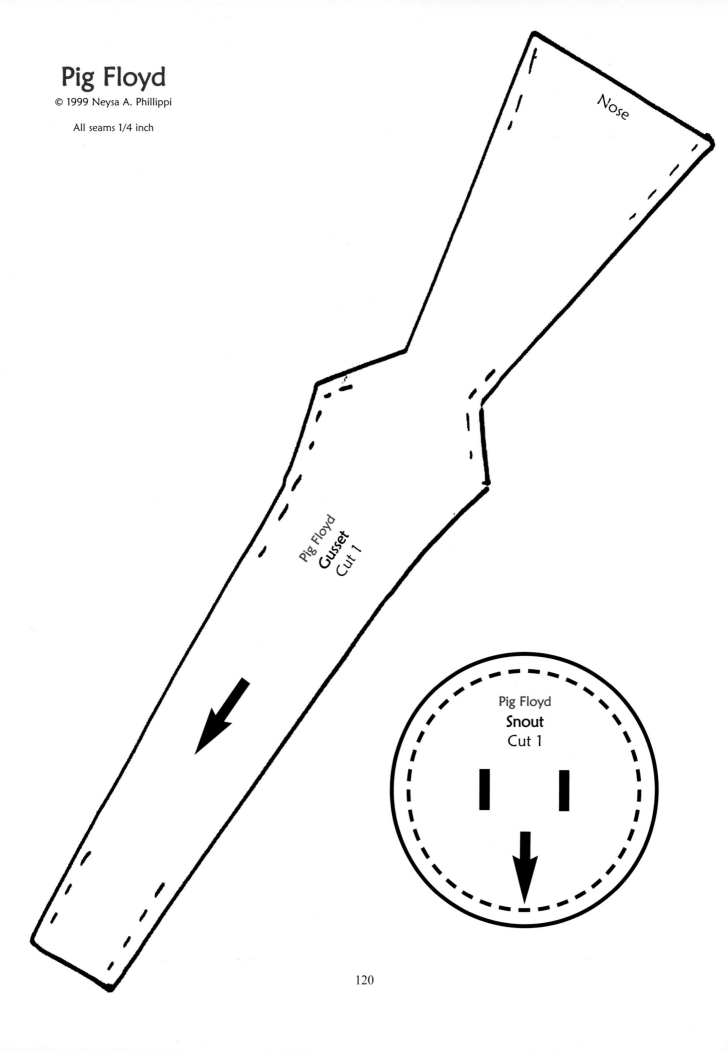

Nose

Pig Floyd
Gusset
Cut 1

Pig Floyd
Snout
Cut 1

120

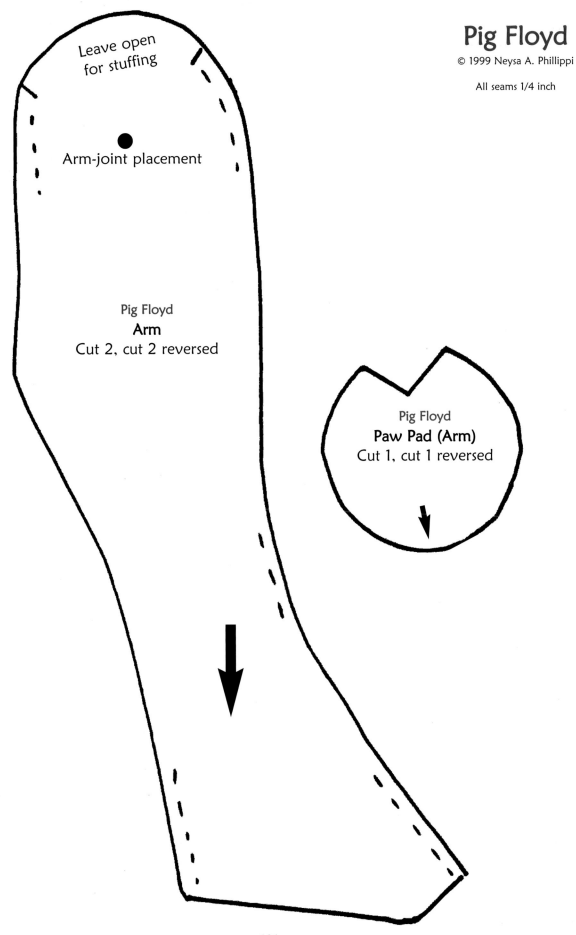

Pig Floyd

© 1999 Neysa A. Phillippi

All seams 1/4 inch

Leave open
for stuffing

Arm-joint placement

Pig Floyd
Arm
Cut 2, cut 2 reversed

Pig Floyd
Paw Pad (Arm)
Cut 1, cut 1 reversed

121

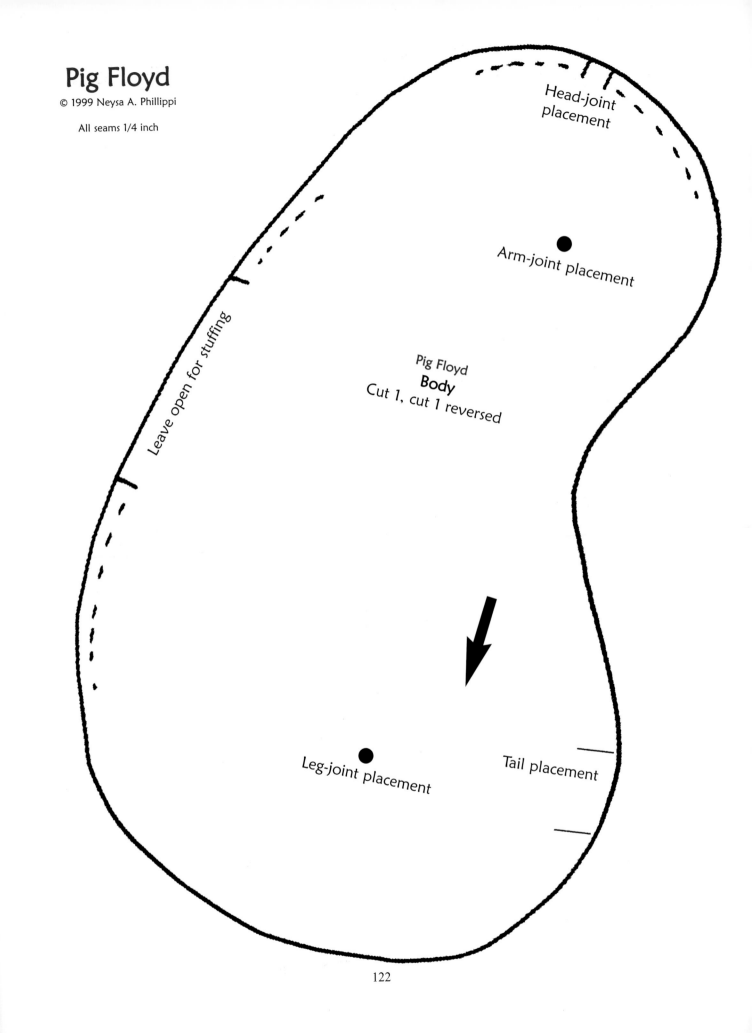

Pig Floyd

© 1999 Neysa A. Phillippi

All seams 1/4 inch

Head-joint placement

Arm-joint placement

Leave open for stuffing

Pig Floyd
Body
Cut 1, cut 1 reversed

Leg-joint placement

Tail placement

122

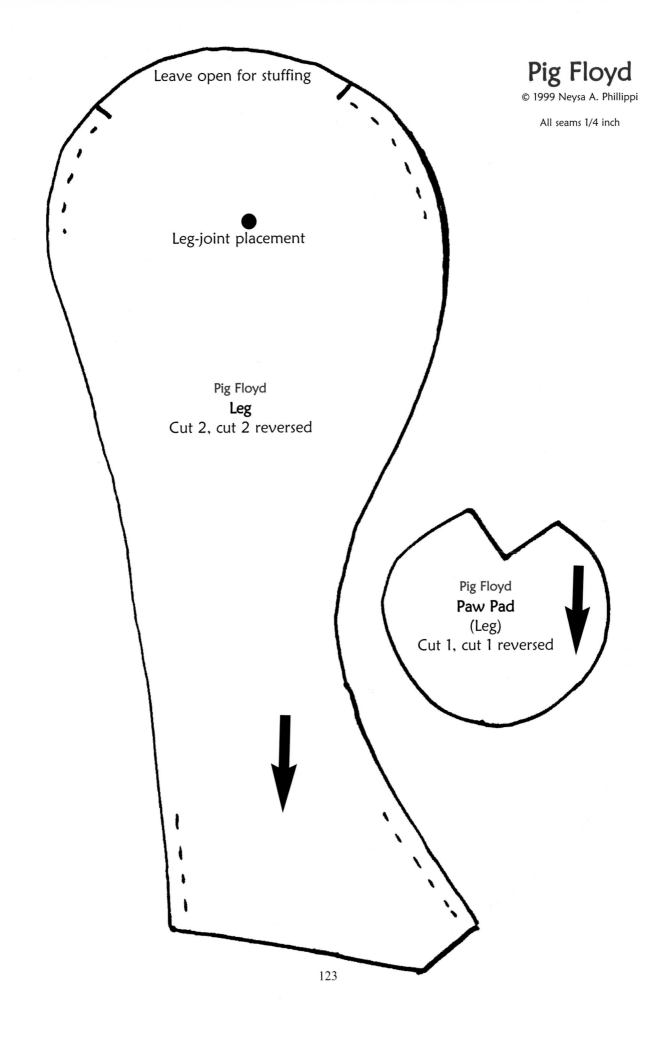

Leave open for stuffing

Pig Floyd

© 1999 Neysa A. Phillippi

All seams 1/4 inch

Leg-joint placement

Pig Floyd
Leg
Cut 2, cut 2 reversed

Pig Floyd
Paw Pad
(Leg)
Cut 1, cut 1 reversed

123

Harvey was named for my favorite Jimmy Stewart movie. He is nineteen inches (48 cm) tall, and has wired ears and a large fluffy tail. Unlike the Harvey in the movie, this rabbit is visible and much more colorful.

Harvey

Harvey is nineteen inches tall.

Materials

- 1/2 yard (30 x 36 inches or 18 x 54 inches) mohair, any style, color and length
- 9-inch-square of velour upholstery fabric, felt, ultra suede or other fabric for paw pads
- 9-inch-square of mohair or plush for Harvey's tail
- 9-inch-square of mohair or plush for Harvey's chest patch (top of body)
- One pair of 9-mm glass or plastic eyes
- Three sets of 35-mm joints and two sets of 45-mm joints
- Yarn for nose and mouth
- Sewing machine thread for seams to match mohair color (if stuffing with pellets, sew all seams twice)
- Nylon upholstery thread for attaching eyes and closing seams
- Floral or fine copper wire for the ears
- Polyester stuffing and plastic pellets

Harvey

54 inches

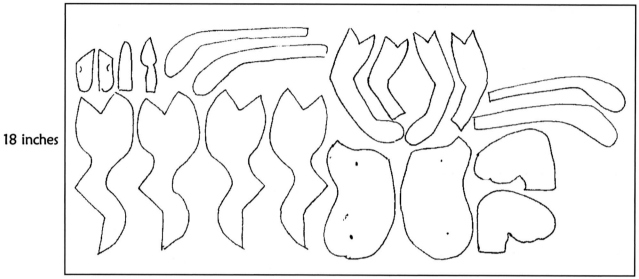

18 inches

1/2 yard (30 x 36 inches or 18 x 54 inches) of mohair or plush needed

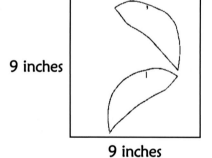

9 inches

9 inches

9-inch-square of
mohair or plush for
the chest patch
(top of body)

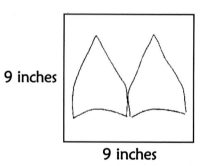

9 inches

9 inches

9-inch-square of
mohair or plush for
Harvey's tail

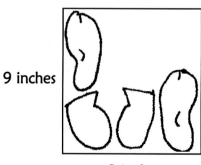

9 inches

9 inches

9-inch-square of
velour, felt or other
fabric for the paw
and foot pads

Directions

Read and follow the basic directions for layout, cutting, pinning and sewing.

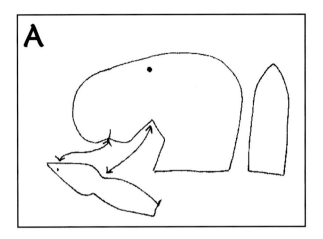

Head: Sew the side head and neck gusset as shown in **Diagram A**; match points and ease the neck gusset into the underside of the side head piece. Sew the other side head to the neck gusset. Then sew the back head gusset to the side heads. Lastly, sew the two side heads together; the head will have a center seam.

Body: Sew a chest patch to a body as pictured in **Diagram B**. Repeat with the other chest patch and body pieces. Then sew the two body pieces together.

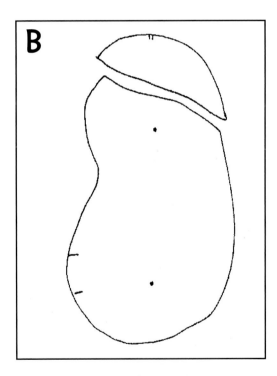

Tail: Hand sew the tail in place after the body is stuffed.

Ears: Hand sew the ears to the head after it is stuffed. The ears can be wired either by sewing floral wire between the two seams or by tacking the wire to critical points on the ears such, as their tips and curves.

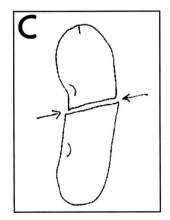

Foot Pads: Harvey has two-piece foot pads, as shown in **Diagram C**. Sew the two pieces together at the arrows, and then attach them to the legs in the normal manner.

To create a floppy rabbit, loosely stuff and joint Harvey.

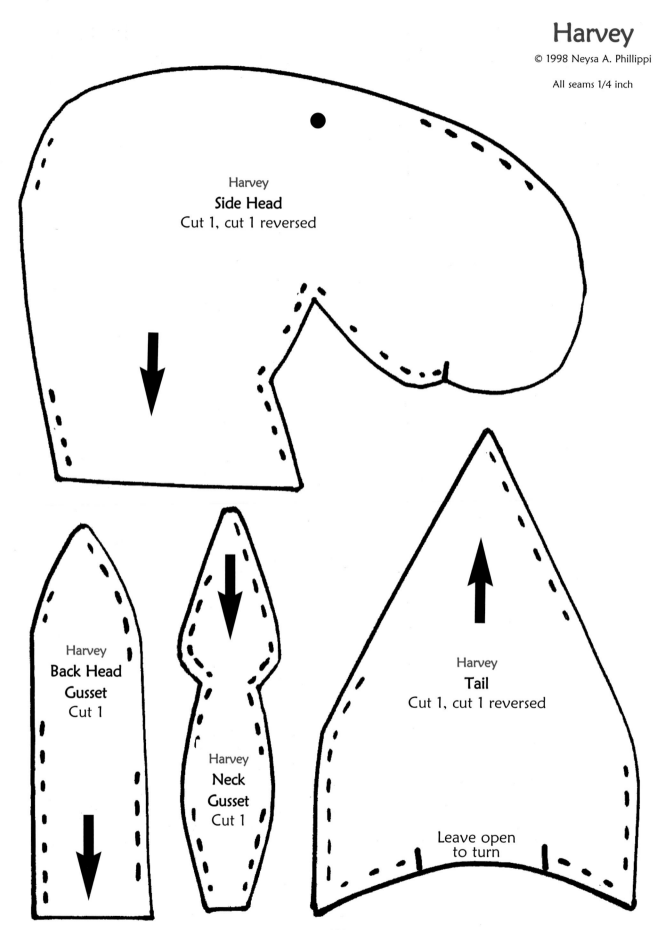

Harvey

All seams 1/4 inch

Harvey
Side Head
Cut 1, cut 1 reversed

Harvey
Back Head
Gusset
Cut 1

Harvey
Neck
Gusset
Cut 1

Harvey
Tail
Cut 1, cut 1 reversed

Leave open
to turn

All seams 1/4 inch

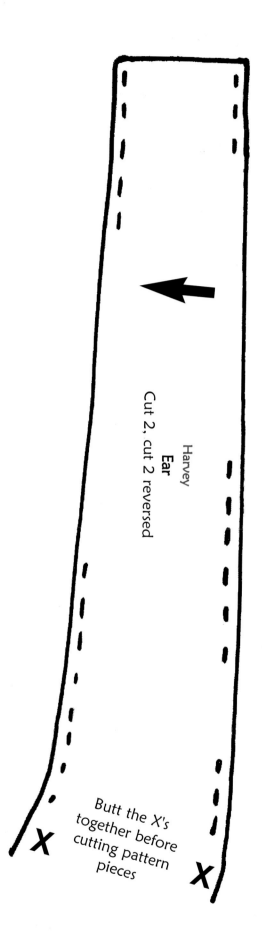

Harvey
Ear
Cut 2, cut 2 reversed

Butt the X's together before cutting pattern pieces

X

X

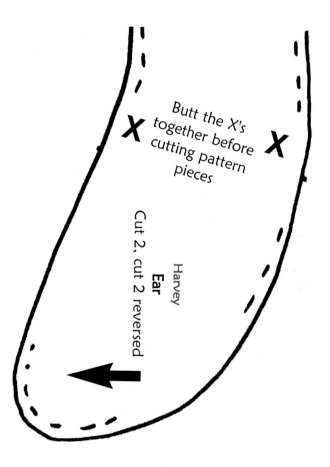

Butt the X's together before cutting pattern pieces

X

X

Harvey
Ear
Cut 2, cut 2 reversed

Harvey's Ear
If you wish to make the underside of the ear from a different fabric, such as the fabric used for the paw pads, cut 1 and cut 1 reversed in each fabric.

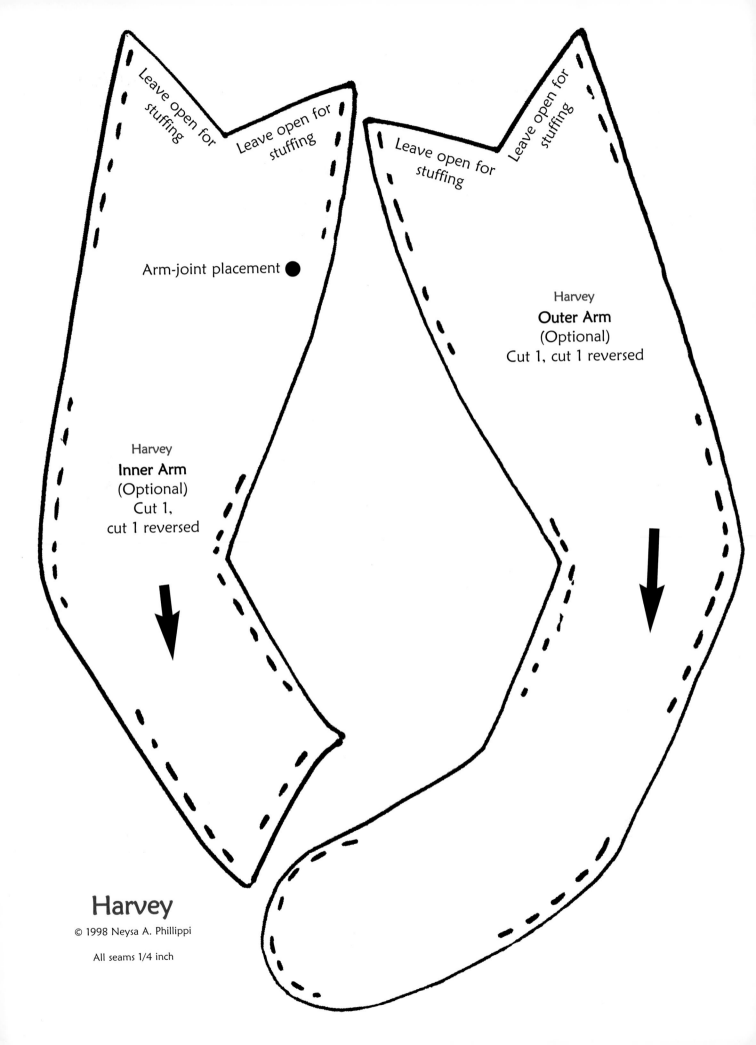

Leave open for stuffing

Leave open for stuffing

Arm-joint placement ●

Harvey
Inner Arm
(Optional)
Cut 1,
cut 1 reversed

Leave open for stuffing

Leave open for stuffing

Harvey
Outer Arm
(Optional)
Cut 1, cut 1 reversed

Harvey

© 1998 Neysa A. Phillippi

All seams 1/4 inch

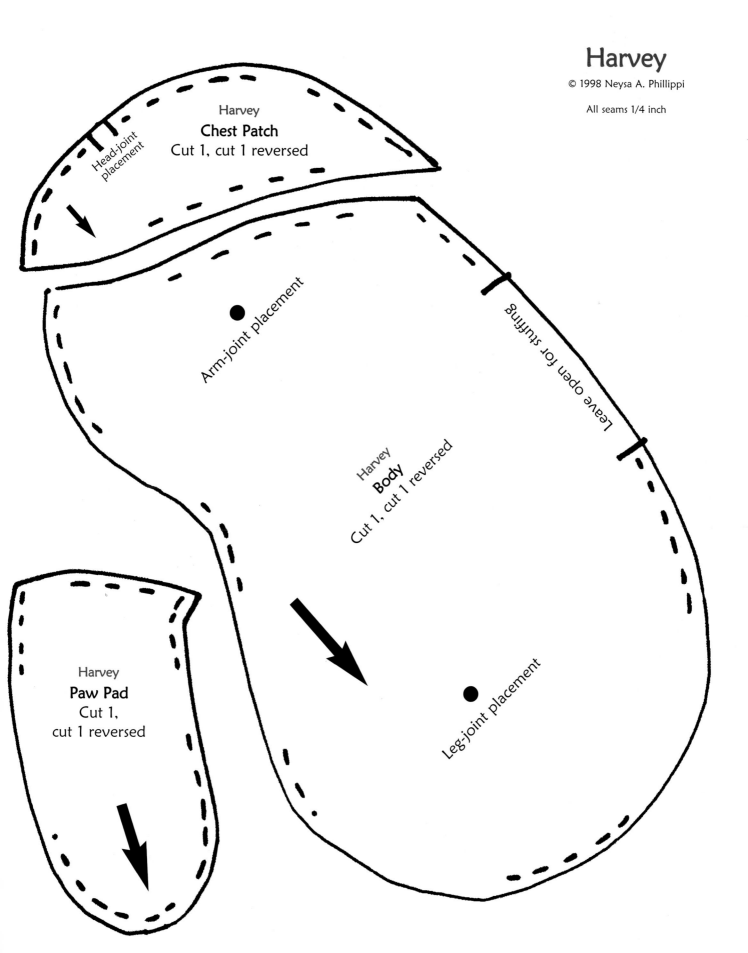

Harvey
© 1998 Neysa A. Phillippi

All seams 1/4 inch

Head-joint placement

Harvey
Chest Patch
Cut 1, cut 1 reversed

Arm-joint placement

Leave open for stuffing

Harvey
Body
Cut 1, cut 1 reversed

Harvey
Paw Pad
Cut 1,
cut 1 reversed

Leg-joint placement

Harvey

© 1998 Neysa A. Phillippi

All seams 1/4 inch

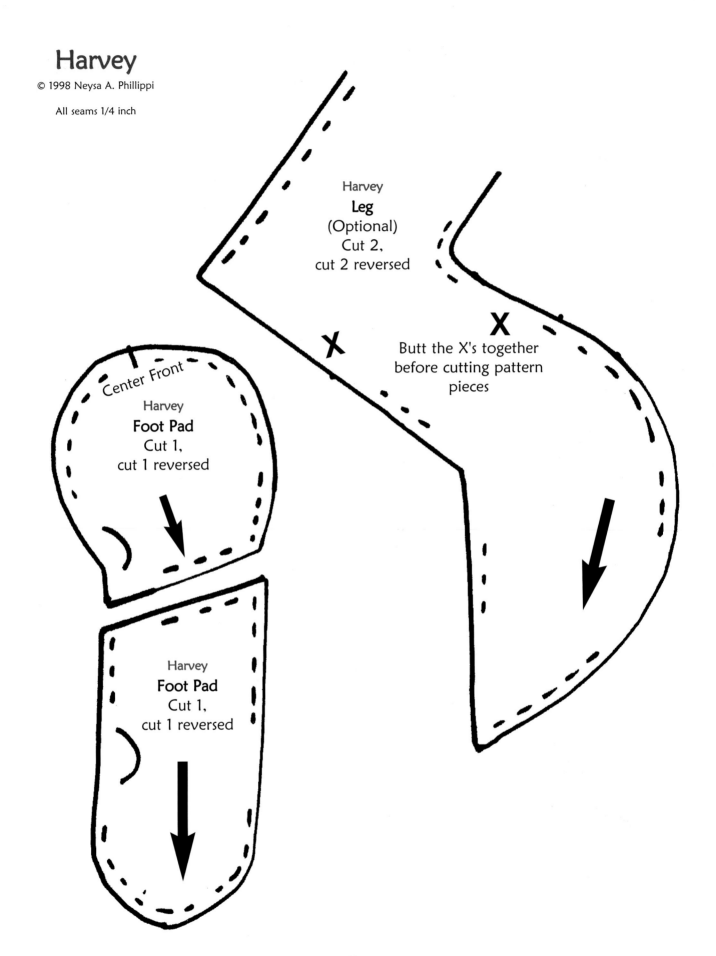

Harvey
Leg
(Optional)
Cut 2,
cut 2 reversed

X   X

Butt the X's together
before cutting pattern
pieces

Center Front

Harvey
Foot Pad
Cut 1,
cut 1 reversed

Harvey
Foot Pad
Cut 1,
cut 1 reversed

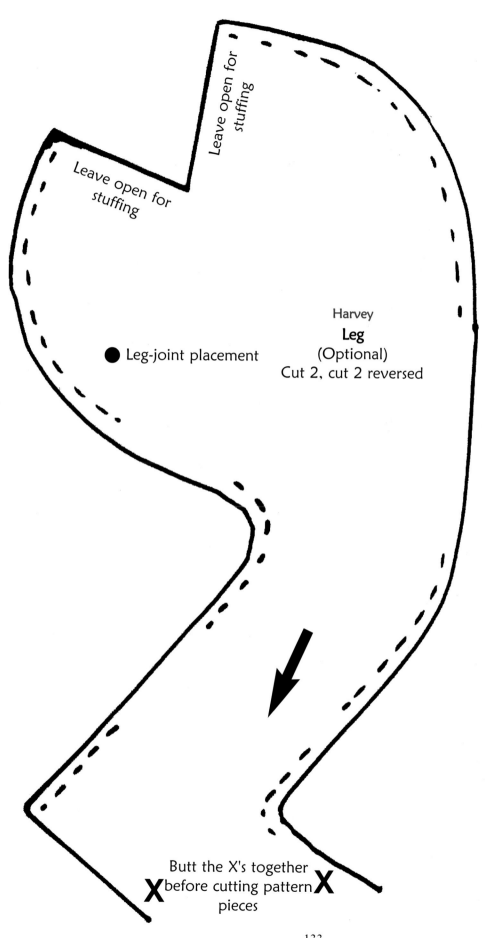

Harvey

All seams 1/4 inch

Leave open for stuffing

Leave open for stuffing

● Leg-joint placement

Harvey
Leg
(Optional)
Cut 2, cut 2 reversed

Butt the X's together before cutting pattern pieces

X   X

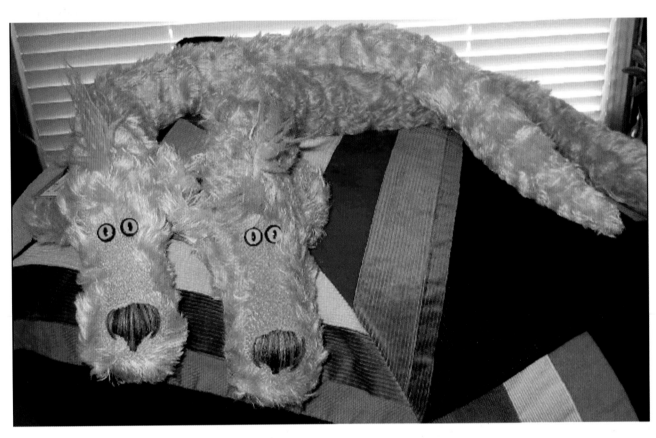

Wiggles Worm (two pictured) is designed to lay across your computer monitor or at your door as a draft dodger. He is thirty-three inches (83 cm) long and very funky with his mohawk. Add an earring and you've created a masterpiece of the "worm kind!"

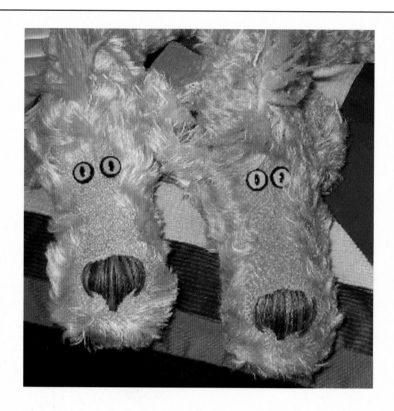

Wiggles Worm

Wiggles Worm is thirty-three inches (83 cm) from his nose to the tip of his body or tail.

Materials

- 12 x 36 inches of mohair or plush if the nap or fur lies flat along the 36-inch length; or 12 x 54 inches of mohair or plush if the fur or nap lays flat along the 54-inch length
- 1¼ x 2½ inches of long mohair or plush for the mohawk
- One pair of 12-mm cat eyes in glass or plastic
- Yarn for the nose
- Sewing machine thread for seams to match color (if stuffing with pellets, sew all seams twice)
- Nylon upholstery thread for attaching eyes and closing seams
- Polyester stuffing and plastic pellets

Wiggles Worm

36 inches

12 inches

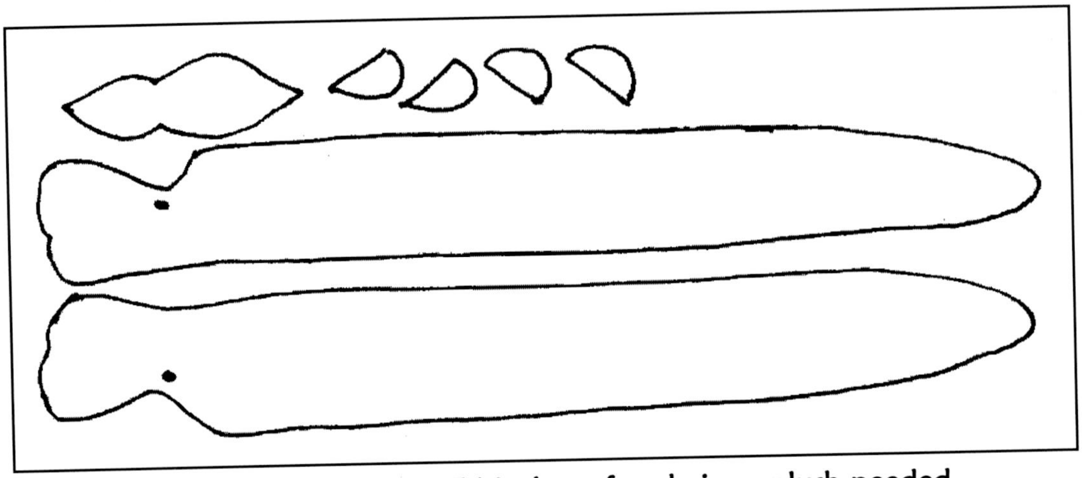

12 x 36 inches or 12 x 54 inches of mohair or plush needed

2½ inches

1¼ inches

1¼ x 2½ inches of long mohair or plush for the mohawk

Wiggles Worm

© 2001 Neysa A. Phillippi

All seams 1/4 inch

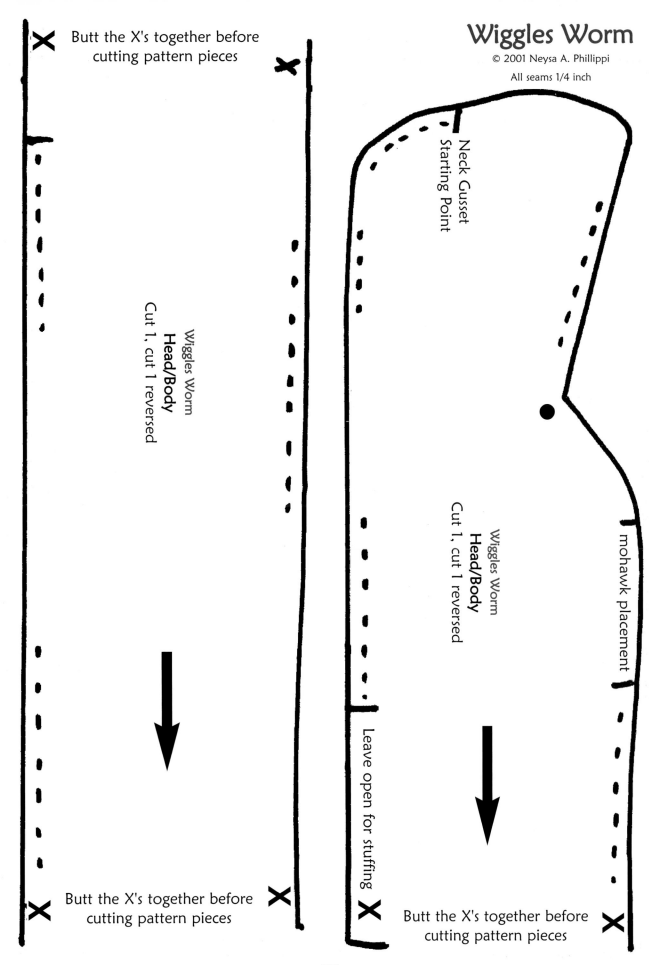

Butt the X's together before cutting pattern pieces

Wiggles Worm
Head/Body
Cut 1, cut 1 reversed

Butt the X's together before cutting pattern pieces

Neck Gusset Starting Point

Wiggles Worm
Head/Body
Cut 1, cut 1 reversed

mohawk placement

Leave open for stuffing

Butt the X's together before cutting pattern pieces

Wiggles Worm

© 2001 Neysa A. Phillippi

All seams 1/4 inch

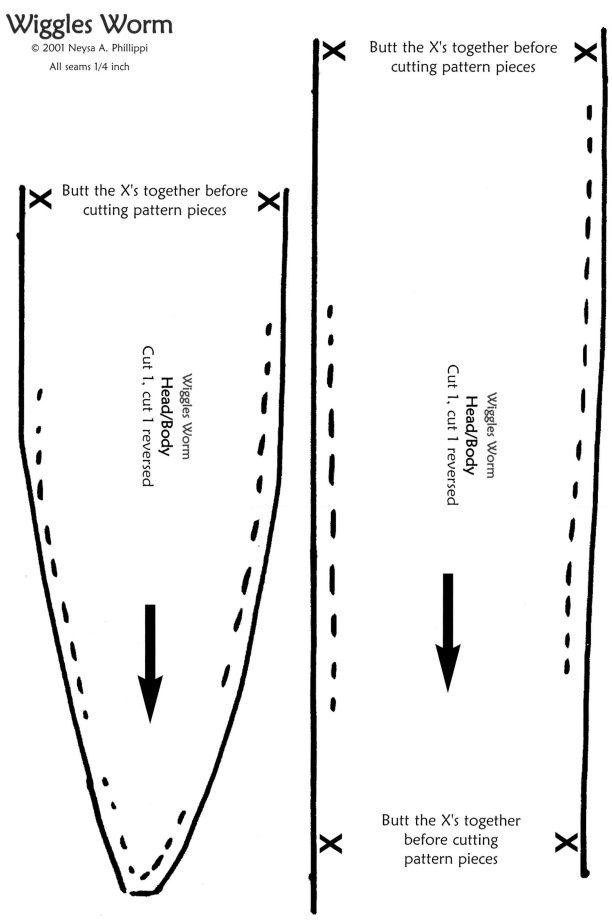

Butt the X's together before cutting pattern pieces

Butt the X's together before cutting pattern pieces

Wiggles Worm
Head/Body
Cut 1, cut 1 reversed

Wiggles Worm
Head/Body
Cut 1, cut 1 reversed

Butt the X's together before cutting pattern pieces

Wiggles Worm
© 2001 Neysa A. Phillippi

All seams 1/4 inch

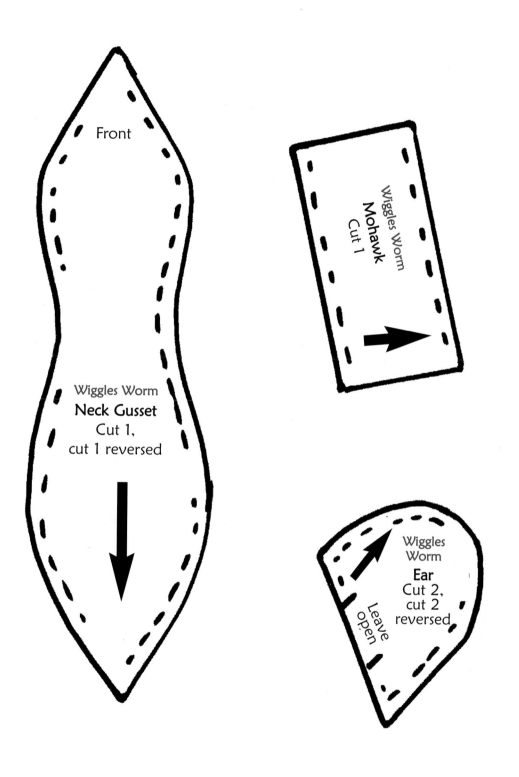

Front

Wiggles Worm

Neck Gusset
Cut 1,
cut 1 reversed

Wiggles Worm
Mohawk
Cut 1

Wiggles
Worm
Ear
Cut 2,
cut 2
reversed

Leave
open

139

Artists' Secrets for Making Better Creatures

Nose Jobs Made Easy. When hand stitching a nose with pearl cotton, stuff the tip of the nose with excelsior first. I hold the excelsior in place either with long stitches through the nose or long needles; either will keep it from sliding out. Then add your stuffing material such as Polyfil, replacing the long needles or adding more long stitches to hold the stuffing in place. When the snout is completely stuffed, start stuffing the head; after it is one-third full, remove the stitches or needles that held the excelsior or stuffing in place in the snout—at this point, it stays put and will not tend to slip out. The excelsior in the tip of the nose allows you to hand embroider the area easily and keeps the nose stitches perfectly aligned. It keeps your wrist from getting tired trying to constantly pull the stitches through the nose—even a pliers to pull the stitches is used less often.

One of the most important things in stitching a nose is to do it under good, direct lighting. I use an overhead clamp light, which allows me to bring the light down directly over my head and the animal's head in my hand. First, using an extra-fine permanent marker, I draw an exact outline of the shape I desire. I draw this just a wee bit smaller than I want the finished nose be. This helps me stitch the shape desired and allows for tiny mistakes in the event the drawing is slightly off center. (You can correct the outline when you stitch the nose, making adjustments as needed.) I 'cross hatch' the stitching by first stitching horizontally. Using pearl cotton, I place my stitches one next to the other until the outline is covered. I then stitch vertically over the horizontal stitches. I do this with extreme care—working carefully in laying each new stitch next to the last one and pulling the thread with even tension on every stitch. I smooth each stitch down by gently rubbing them with the tip of my fingers.

I use an old brown candle—buy one with the whitish coating on it—broken into two-inch to three-inch pieces for easy handling. After the nose is perfectly stitched, I lightly rub the edge of the candle over the pearl cotton stitches, going with the direction of the threads from end to end. I then blow on the palm of my hand and lightly rub the warmed palm gently over the waxed stitches, once again going in the direction of the stitches, end to end. On small noses, I use my breath-warmed fingertips. I do this from two to six times: applying the wax candle on the stitches and rubbing with my warmed palm or fingers. The number of candle-wax applications and rubs is determined by how "waxy" and vintage you want the nose to look.—**Karen A. Meer, The Mad Hatted Bear, meer2@execpc.com**

Stuck on Noses. I use a paintbrush to add a small dab of watered-down tacky glue to the area where the animal's nose will be. The glue holds the yarn in place, and the creature's nose will never separate. Tacky glue will wash out, and it dries clear. You should use it sparingly, however; if you use too much, it will seep through the yarn and make a hard spot.—**Neysa A. Phillippi**

Ear, Ear. Here's how to create what I call my "Three-Stitch Ear": After threading your needle, attach the thread to the head gusset where you want the top of the ear to be positioned. Then run your needle through the top of the ear, and run the thread back through the head gusset where you came out with your first stitch. Next, run the needle out of the side head where the other end of the ear will be attached, attach the thread to the ear and run the needle back into the side head where your needle came out. Pull your needle out in the middle of these two stitches, but slightly more to the back of the head (to make a cupped ear). Run your needle through the center of the ear, and then back into the head where your needle came out. Pull the thread tightly and securely. Repeat for the other ear. —Celia Baham, Celia's Teddies, Celiasteds@aol.com

Handy Helpers.
My favorite tools of the trade are: (1) a Sunbeam Steam Valet—a jet of steam directed to the fur that is either unruly or going the wrong direction can style and change the appearance of your bear or other stuffed animal. After steaming and redirecting the fur with a fingertip brush, use Scotch tape to hold it in place until the fur is dry. (2) Trimming shears—approximately five inches in size. Be sure to purchase top-quality shears from a beauty supply house. Fur can be trimmed around the face, on top of the nose, etc., and won't have that chopped look of scissors-cut fur.—Virginia Jasmer, Jazzbears, Jazzbears@ix.Netcom.com

Close Shave.
Hate trimming your creature's muzzles with scissors? Buy a beard and mustache trimmer, such as the Norelco Maverick T-3000. It has a smaller trimmer attached that works for small areas and a larger trimmer for the tops of the muzzle. The T-3000 is battery/electrically operated. Your local beauty supply house should have similar small trimmers that will work well. Need something for large areas? Try dog-grooming trimmers; I use them to trim my rats' tails and legs.—Neysa A. Phillippi

Stay in Line.
When putting a nose and mouth on a creature with the center seam on the side nose area a little off, center the mouth with the center of the gusset between the placement of the eyes. This will give you the line you need to follow.—Celia Baham, Celia's Teddies, Celiasteds@aol.com

Accentuate the Positive.
To create the illusion of airbrushing, use Prisma oil pencils. You can create highlights and shadows by using light and dark colors. Remove any excess pencil oil with a cosmetic sponge. Areas to work on: the inside of the ear, the outer ear, the eye socket, around the nose and mouth, and cheek blush.—Robert Zacher, Robert Zacher Originals, BobZacherBears@aol.com

Oh Buy Glass, by Golly.
Glass pellets are great to use as they give weight to your creations. Pellets in feet allow the animals to stand on their own.—Donna Nielsen, Cookies Critters, ccritter@frontiernet.net

Stuff It.
Looking for steel shot? Find someone who sandblasts; steel shot is what they use. It comes in different sizes and varies from ruff to smooth and round.

Buying plastic pellets? The larger the amount you buy, the cheaper by the pound it is. Call a friend and order together. Try General Polymer, a division of Ashland Chemical.

Have the name of a supplier but don't have its number? Call 00 info or 411 to get the number and find out if you can get a better price.—Neysa A. Phillippi

Smart Pinning and Sewing.
When pinning pieces, use two colors of pins—one color for where to sew and the other color to tell you when to stop sewing; this helps in preventing that tiresome mistake of sewing the "openings" closed.

After sewing seams, pick all the mohair from the seams, then 'pink' the edges. This allows for smooth curves and reduces bulk—especially in pointy little cat ears. Use armatures in cats' tails to make posing easy. If making an elephant, wire its trunk so it will hold its position.—**Judith Eppolito, Ashenberry Collectibles, ashbry@aiusa.com**

The Pro's Knot In.
For a smoother finish when closing your seams or stitching on ears, pull all knots to the inside.—**Neysa A. Phillippi**

Rip Tip.
When repairing a rip on an old bear or creature (or a new one), I always put muslin in the back of the repair area. I use a piece that is at least two inches bigger then the area being repaired, and attach it. This gives support to the stitches and will not rip out old mohair.—**Celia Baham, Celia's Teddies, Celiasteds@aol.com**

Personal Colors.
If you want to make a different creature from what you see at shows, try dying your mohair. Start with a white or natural color and use liquid dyes; liquid dyes are easier to measure, and thus make it easier for you to get the same color again. Dye wetted mohair in a tub, turning it several times so you get an even color throughout the mohair. Try mixing colors in a measuring cup, coming up with a variety of colors not even on the market. Happy Coloring!—**Terry Hayes, Pendleton's Teddy Bears, pendletonsteddy@adelphia.net**

Recycling Steps.
When working with real fur, you should always first check the pelts to make sure that there are no splits or that dry rot hasn't taken place. If the pelt is dry rotted, it will be very brittle and will easily fall apart. Once you have determined that it is workable, a lining such as muslin or even the lining that was in the garment to begin with will work. Cut your pattern out of the lining and then out of the fur. Baste your lining to the fur, and then stitch the pieces together as normal. I don't recommend using a fusible lining because the number one rule with real fur is 'do not place in, near, or around heat.' Ironing in a fusible lining could create dry rot down the road. If you omit the task of lining a real-fur animal, you will end up with seams that pop and, possibly, pieces that are impossible to turn right side out.—**Dina Denning, Creative Stitches by Dina, Inc., dina@dinadenn.com**

Bright Bite.
If you want to make teeth for rabbits and mice, use Fimo clay (off white). Shape it into a triangle, flatten it, and then use a toothpick to press down center to indent between teeth. Bake at 230 degrees for twenty minutes. To attach to a critter, poke a hole with an awl where the mouth will be. Squeeze Jewel-brand glue into the hole, then push the top end of the teeth into the hole; let dry overnight.—**Darlene Formanek, Bearmaker's Cottage, Bearmaker726@yahoo.com**

Getting Around the Joint.
If you have one joint that you can't get as tight as the rest, try a rubber band between the body and the uncooperative arm or leg. Do this after the creature is finished.
—**Neysa A. Phillippi**

There is no right or wrong way to make a bear, cat, rat or other creature. Never be afraid to ask others how or why they do what they do!

Invaluable Sources
for supplies, patterns, books and tours

SUPPLIES

Artemis
179 High St.
South Portland, ME 04106
Tel 888 233-5187
Fax 207 741-2497
Email: artemis@ime.net
Hand-dyed, bias-cut Hannah silk and
satin ribbon

Bear Street - Dale Junker
415 W. Foothill Blvd.
Claremont, CA 91711
Tel. 909 625-2995
Mohair, eyes, joints, patterns, kits

Bolek's Craft Supplies
P.O. Box 465
330 N. Tuscarawas Ave.
Dover, OH 44622-0465
Tel 330 364-8878; 800 743-2723
Fax 800 649-3735
Plastic joints and other craft supplies

Dollspart Supply Company, Inc.
The Teddy Works
8000 Cooper Ave., Bldg. 28
Glendale, NY 11385
Tel 1 800 336-DOLL
Fax 718 326-4971
Teddy bear and doll supplies, joints,
eyes, etc.

Enterprise Art
2860 Roosevelt Blvd.
Clearwater, FL 34620
Craft supplies

Golden Fun Kits
PO Box 10697
Edgemont Branch
Golden, CO 80401-0600
Eyes, music boxes,
patterns, etc.
(Mail-order only)

Intercal Trading Group
1760 Monrovia Ave.,
Ste. A-17
Costa Mesa, CA 92627
Tel 949 645-9396
Fax 949 645-5471
www.intercaltg.com
Mohair, eyes, etc.

The Leather Factory
2435 W. Pawnee
PO Box 13100
Wichita, KS 67213
Tel 559 942-7773
1 800 984-7147
Leather, rivets, etc.

L.Z. Products
Attention: Ivy Tuber
2121 W. 21st St.
Chicago, IL 60608
Tel 773 847-0572
Fax 773 847-1171
Ultra suede, velour upholstery fabric

Monterey Mills
PO Box 271
Janesville, WI 53547
Tel 608 754-2866
Fax 608 754-3750
Fake fur (knit), stuffing (Quality A is
about $1.85 a pound in 20 pound
bags; minimum order $100)

Name Maker, Inc.
PO Box 43821
Atlanta, GA 30378-3601
Tel 1 800 241-2890
Fax 404 691-7711
Fabric name tags

Newark Dressmaker Supply
6473 Ruch Road
PO Box 20730
Lehigh Valley, PA 18002-0730
Tel 800 736-6783
Thread, needles, etc.

North State Supply Co, Inc.
390 Fergesen Road
Homer City, PA 15748
Tel. 724 479-3511
Cotter pins, bolts, nuts, pop rivets and
pop rivet guns in volume for great
prices

Purely Neysa
45 Gorman Ave.
Indiana, PA 15701-2244 USA
Tel 724 349-1225
Fax 724 349-3903
Email: neysa@purelyneysa.com
www.purelyneysa.com
Patterns, books, needle felting supplies,
woven Belgium plush, eyes and more

Reinhold Lesch GmbH
Oeslauer StraBe 121-123
D-96472 Rodental
Germany
Tel 011 49 95 63 72 21 0
Fax 011 49 95 63 72 21 22
www.Lesch.de
Eyes, growlers, doll wigs

Sandy's Victorian Trims
7417 North Knoxville Avenue
Peoria, IL 61614
Tel 309 689-1943
Fax 309 689-1942
Silk ribbon

Sierra Meadows Bears
PO Box 90309
Long Beach, CA 90809-0309
Tel 562 981-8882; 866 MYFURRY
Fax 562 982-8868
www.bearsandbooks.com
Info@bearsandbooks.com
Books, patterns, kits and needles of
all kinds

Standard Doll Co.
23-83 31st St.
Long Island City, NY 11105
Tel 800 543-6557
Fax 718 274-4231

Tandy Leather & Craft
800 555-3130 (Call for a catalog)

PATTERNS

Celia's Teddies
Celia Baham
1562 San Joaquin Ave.
San Jose, CA 95118
Tel 408 266-8129
Email: Celiasteds@aol.com
www.Celiasteddies.com
Bears, cats and patterns

Creative Design
Roberta Kasnick Ripperger
PO Box 1381
Elmhurst, IL 60126
Tel 630 834-2073
Fax 630 834-1104
www. Beyond-basic-bears.com
Email: rkr4cds@attbi.com
Miniature bears, patterns and fabrics

Invaluable Sources *continued*

BOOKS

Animal Encyclopedia
By Barbara Taylor
Dorling Kindersley, 2000

Animal Portraits
By Walter Schels (photographer) and
Dennis C. Turner
Publishers Group West, 2001

Animals on White
By Pete Dine (photographer) and
Markus Mader
Publishers Group West, 2001

A Zoology of the Future After Man
By Dougal Dixon
St. Martin's Press, 1981

**Barron's Encyclopedia of Cat Breeds:
A Complete Guide to the Domestic
Cats of North America**
By J. Anne Helgren
Barrons Education Series, 1997

The Big Book of Cats
By Alan Edwards and
Grace McHattie
PRC Publishing Ltd., 1999

The Book of the Cat
Edited by Michael Wright and
Sally Walters
Summit Books, 1980

**The Complete Chicken: An
Entertaining History of Chickens**
By Pam Percy
Voyageur Press, 2002

Constructing TEDDY and His Friends
By Jennifer Laing
Hobby House Press, Inc., 2002

The Encyclopedia of Mammals
Edited by Dr. David Macdonald
Equinox (Oxford) Ltd., 1984

**Encyclopedia of Reptiles and
Amphibians, A Comprehensive
Illustrated Guide by International
Experts**
Consulting Editors Dr. Harold G.
Cogger and Dr. Richard D. Zweisl
Fog City Press, 1998 Second Edition

The Last of the Wild Horses
By Martin Harbury
Arrowood Press, 1989

Legacy of the Cat
By Gloria Stephens
Chronicle Books, 1990

**National Geographic Animal
Encyclopedia**
By The National Geographic Society
National Geographic Society, 2000

**The Simon & Schuster Encyclopedia of
Animals: A Visual Who's Who of the
World's Creatures**
By Philip Whitfield
Simon & Schuster, 1998

Smithsonian Handbooks: Cats
By David Alderton, Marc Henrie (photographer) and Daphne Negus
Dorling Kindersley Publishing, Inc.,
2002

**Smithsonian Institution ANIMAL
The Definitive Visual Guide to the
World's Wildlife**
Editors-in-Chief David Burnie & Don E.
Wilson
Dorling Kindersley Publishing, Inc.,
2001

The Ultimate Guide to Horse Breeds
By Andrea Fitzpatrick
Chartwell Books, 2003

Wild Animals of North America
By The National Geographic Society
National Geographic Society, 1979

COLLECTOR TOURS

Neysa A. Phillippi Presenter
OFF THE WALL Creative Tours
(Featuring the "Artists for Artists"
Annual European Tours & Antique
Market Tours)
45 Gorman Ave.
Indiana, PA 15701-2244
Tel 724 349-1225
Fax 724 349-3903
Email:
offthewalltours@purelyneysa.com
www.purelyneysa.com